PRAI
SECRETS (

Jamie Galloway is a spiritual son of whom I am very proud and excited to see him writing. His new book, *Secrets of the Seer,* is rich in revelation for anyone with a desire to be used of God in the prophetic/seer realm. It brings wisdom to those who take the opportunity to grow by reading *Secrets of the Seer.* I believe Jamie's writings will open up your understanding of the ways of God, especially in the revelatory realm. Thank you, Jamie, for your strong gift and anointing, for your walking in integrity all these eighteen years that I have known you. Glad to see you putting into writing the things you have learned in your life in the prophetic-seer realm. I know many others will have new breakthroughs as they discover for themselves, as they read, what God has taught you.

Blessings,

—RANDY CLARK, D. MIN.
Overseer of the Apostolic Network of Global Awakening,
founder of Global Awakening.

God is about to change our normal. One way is activating our ability to see into the unseen world. Jamie Galloway is raised up by God to supernaturally help open your spiritual eyes. James 5:19 says Jesus ONLY did what He SAW the Father doing! That's the new norm!

—SID ROTH
Host, *It's Supernatural TV*

In every generation there are quality voices the Holy Spirit raises up within the Body of Christ. They carry integrity in their character, authenticity in their gifting, and maturity in their relationships. I have known Jamie Galloway for over twenty years and have observed his growth in all of these arenas of life and ministry. It is now my honor to commend to you his prophetic insights in *Secrets of the Seer*.

JAMES W. GOLL
Founder of God Encounters Ministries

Jamie Galloway is one of God's hand-picked instruments of grace in a day when there is a need for a fresh awareness of the vital, animating presence of the Holy Spirit in the work of the Church as God's prophetic instrument in the earth. The charisms—despite the argument of cessationists—have continued through the ages in those who have honored the work of the Spirit in their lives to graciously bestow such manifestations of Himself. I am deeply touched by the way Jamie has allowed himself to be available to the Lord to be used in ways that demonstrate the Spirit's power. It is quite refreshing! This new book, *Secrets of the Seer*, will make you hungry for a fresh outpouring of the Spirit in your life so that by abiding in Christ and abiding in His Word, you can see the unseen, hear the unheard, and speak the unspoken! Feast at the table the Lord has spread through Jamie's obedience and availability to Him!

—DR. MARK J. CHIRONNA
Mark Chironna Ministries
Church On The Living Edge
Longwood, Florida

Jamie Galloway's *Secrets of the Seer* is a very necessary read. Jamie's practical and spiritual 10 steps will help you recognize what is happening in the spirit realm around you. I highly value Jamie and have personally learned from him.

—Robby Dawkins
Author, Conference Speaker, Film and TV personality

When I first met Jamie Galloway, I didn't quite know what to make of him. He's very much a seer, and as I am decidedly not, I always felt like he knew a lot more than he was letting on, or that I was somehow missing something that was, of course, obvious to him in the spiritual world. But then he became one of my better friends, and I wasn't just seeing Jamie from behind a camera lens, but I was now getting to know his heart and who he truly was when he wasn't on stage speaking or ministering. And that heart is a big one, and he is exactly the same man off stage that he is on it. He is a humble, loving, big-hearted guy who loves his family and people well, which is far more impressive to me than any spiritual gift he brings to the table. And those spiritual gifts are amazing. I've known quite a few seers over the years, and the danger many of them face is allowing their experience and gift to sometimes overshadow their love and application of God's Word in their lives. This is decidedly not the case with Jamie, who loves and knows the Word of God better than most people I know. That being the case, I have no doubt that this book in your hands will speak richly to you, take you to deeper places of solid, Biblical understanding, and move you further into the understanding of who you truly are in Christ.

—Darren Wilson
Founder, CEO WP Films

What an absolute privilege and honor it is to be included in Christ and to fully experience the only true *secret* of life! Thirteen years ago I was a successful multi-millionaire rockstar, but I was also blind, foolish, and incredibly lost. When I found myself at the height of my deplorable pride, God's priceless mercy invited me to gaze into the realm of the afterlife through Christ!

I was given an amazing gift, but can I be totally honest with you? I want more! And in Christ there is always more!

Jamie Galloway is one of today's modern spiritual leaders who infuses my hunger for more. In his new book, *Secrets of the Seer*, Jamie will awaken a godly jealousy in each of us to see deeper into the secret realms of the kingdom. The hidden manuscripts have been given to humanity to unlock the secret doors, gates, and portals, but it is up to us to search these matters out. *Secrets of the Seer* will stir such a hunger in you that I can promise you this: one read will not be enough!

—Brian "Head" Welch,
Co-founder of the band Korn
and *New York Times* bestselling author of
Save Me From Myself, Stronger,
and *With My Eyes Wide Open*

I would like to highly recommend Jamie Galloway's new book, *Secrets of the Seer*. This book will open the eyes of your heart into the mysteries of God's love for us which will release an activation of seeing in the Spirit. I highly suggest anybody who desires to see into heaven, or have encounters in God's glory to read this book as it will inspire as well as impart an anointing to know God more.

—Jerame Nelson, author of *Encountering Angels* and
Burning Ones: Calling Forth a Generation of Dread Champions

Jesus had a knack for turning seekers and skeptics into seers. Nathaniel went from "I'll believe it when I see it" to seeing the heavens open. Jamie Galloway has a similar gift. His book *Secrets of the Seer* will help the seeker and skeptic alike to understand unseen realities of Heaven. I highly recommend this book!

—Bob Hazlett
Author of *The Roar* and *Think Like Heaven*
www.bobhazlett.org

"Seer"—a word that is misunderstood and maligned in many places, but celebrated in Scripture. A seer is more than one who sees stuff, they live revelation. Things they see, experiences they have, circumstances they find themselves in, and enigmas they find themselves unraveling all become part of a tapestry that reveals what God is communicating to them and through them to the people He loves. Jamie Galloway is a seer in the true sense of the word! I have been around the prophetic movement for nearly twenty years and been friends with many seers and heard multiple teachings about what it takes to "see". This book, *Secrets of the Seer*, is the best teaching on the 'what' and 'how' of being a seer I have encountered. I highly recommend it to anyone desiring to grow more in prophetic gifting or anyone curious about what it is like to live a supernatural lifestyle where the veil between the spiritual and the physical realm is thin. It is born out of experience, study, and revelatory wisdom; it comes from one that lives the life he teaches about.

In His love,

—John E. Thomas
Streams Ministries
www.streamsministries.com

SECRETS

OF THE *Seer*

10 KEYS TO ACTIVATING
SEER ENCOUNTERS

JAMIE GALLOWAY

DESTINY IMAGE® PUBLISHERS, INC.

P.O. Box 310, Shippensburg, PA 17257-0310

"Promoting Inspired Lives."

This book and all other Destiny Image and Destiny Image Fiction books are available at Christian bookstores and distributors worldwide.

Cover design by Eileen Rockwell
Interior design by Terry Clifton

For more information on foreign distributors, call 717-532-3040.

Or reach us on the Internet: www.destinyimage.com

ISBN 13 TP: 978-0-7684-1808-8
ISBN 13 EBook: 978-0-7684-1809-5
ISBN LP: 978-0-7684-1810-1
ISBN HC: 978-0-7684-1811-8

For Worldwide Distribution, Printed in the U.S.A.

3 4 5 6 / 20 19 18

CONTENTS

Foreword 1

CHAPTER 1   The Seer's Secret .7

CHAPTER 2   The Secret of Heaven on Earth 25

CHAPTER 3   The Secret of Entertaining Angels. 37

CHAPTER 4   The Secret of Imagination 55

CHAPTER 5   The Secret of the Senses 69

CHAPTER 6   The Secret of Humanity 87

CHAPTER 7   The Secret of Stillness 109

CHAPTER 8   The Secret of Sound. 129

CHAPTER 9   The Secret of Abundance. 141

CHAPTER 10   The Secret of Words 153

CHAPTER 11   The Secret of Dreaming. 165

CHAPTER 12   Activation of Seer Revelation 179

Notes. 185

FOREWORD

*T*his book is going to both help people understand keys to living as one who is gifted as a seer, but it will also provide a platform of faith to every believer who hears from God to make spiritual connections that will build a deeper life in God. It is a book about the power of one of God's roles He has for His people to play in these days: The role of a Seer. The whole world is paying money for life coaches, psychics, and advisors in many fields to solve problems that have a spiritual root system behind the very real problem.

I remember walking into a new age fair where we were doing an outreach. I watched one medium who was claiming to communicate with people's dead relatives, and as she shared from a very real place of wanting to bring encouragement from the supernatural realm, I realized two things:

1. She was encouraging but not resolving anything.

2. She was not ministering to the real issues in the people's hearts concerning the relationships with those she was "contacting."

Sometimes they had an emotional connection, but there wasn't resolution or change. It made me even hungrier for what can happen when we have a genuine connection to Jesus as the source of our spiritual journey.

God had an original and intended design of the world around us and for humanity that bears His image. Romans 8:29-30 says:

> *God knew what he was doing from the very beginning. He decided from the outset to shape the lives of those who love him along the same lines as the life of his Son. The Son stands first in the line of humanity he restored. We see the original and intended shape of our lives there in him. After God made that decision of what his children should be like,*

he followed it up by calling people by name. After he called them by name, he set them on a solid basis with himself. And then, after getting them established, he stayed with them to the end, gloriously completing what he had begun (MSG).

For a basic definition of those who are seers, they are the ones who are looking for God's original intention, and when they see something that is not spiritually in line, they call for alignment. They help resolve spiritual issues because they can see not just the issue through discernment, but they can also see the original plan of God over the situation. They can see God's current heart, and they help pray or prophesy the current situation to manifest God's desire. They can see the secrets of His heart and they help to bridge the gap so that the situation has an invitation to come into its God-given destiny.

We have this contrast between how God worked before the resurrection of Jesus, and how he worked after. Before we had thousands of years where God was promising that there would be a full restoration to His original plan, and that humanity would once again have a chance to have relationship with God the way we were designed to. There were seers and prophets in the Bible who had spectacular encounters with God, and they were known in whole nations. People would go to them when seeking breakthrough, counsel, wisdom, and insight. They were sought out by royalty, famous people, educators, philosophers, and more.

Then Jesus comes and after His death and resurrection, many believers have minimized the incredible role of those who are called to live the life of a seer. The New Testament and the resurrection did not diminish the need for seers; it released us all to a degree into this awesome spiritual ministry to the world.

At the same time, there are those who are called to be seers as a main focus of their passion and heart, and I believe God wants to restore the dignity to their function and role in the world around us. Just like presidents and movie stars are going to psychics for spiritual counsel, we need to let the world around us know God has secrets to reveal. He is powerful and speaks to His friends, and we can then manifest His voice to the world around us.

I love that this book by Jamie Galloway has practical tools from a man who has lived as a seer to help bring perspective to bridging those gaps between God's original intention and the world we live in. Jamie takes us, the readers, through keys to developing a healthy spiritual seer life, such as partnering with the angelic, understanding the imagination, and stewarding our humanity. These are profound keys from a man who has lived a profound life.

I believe that you are about to go on a journey as you read this book. Jamie's very real spiritual encounters and stories are going to be a practical guide to build your faith and answer some big questions about how to pursue the God of mysteries who wants to share His secrets with you.

—SHAWN BOLZ
www.bolzministries.com
Author of *God Secrets, Translating God, Keys to Heaven's Economy*

CHAPTER

1

THE SEER'S SECRET

Moreover the word of the Lord came to me, saying, "Jeremiah, what do you see?" And I said, "I see a branch of an almond tree." Then the Lord said to me, "You have seen well, for I am ready to perform My word."

—JEREMIAH 1:11-12

Observe, first, dear friends, that before Jeremiah becomes a speaker for God, he must be a seer. The name for a prophet, in the olden time, was a "seer"—a man who could see, one who could see with his mind's eye, one who could also see with spiritual insight, so as vividly to realize the truth which he had to deliver in the name of the Lord. Learn that simple lesson well, O you who try to speak for God! You must be seers before you can be speakers.

—CHARLES SPURGEON,
"The Lesson of the Almond Tree"

*I*t was a family vacation. We had several days of Disney planned, and my kids were looking forward to every moment. I might have been a bit excited as well, but by the end of the first day, after dealing with the terribly long lines, I was exhausted. This vacation started off with enough walking in one day to fill my quota for the entire month. I was grateful but looking forward to some more relaxing time with my family.

The following day we went to the pool. It was a massive resort pool fully equipped with slides, water volleyball, a lazy river, and all sorts water-related fun. While the kids were enjoying the water playground, I was ready to get some sun. We strapped a life jacket on my four-year-old son and let him run around in the shallow kids' pool. We were set. My wife and I were enjoying some vitamin D from the sun. We were finally relaxing together. This was my kind of vacation. At the time, we were in the middle of a move to a different state so we were thrilled to take some time as a family to regroup and make some wonderful memories together. In the middle of this transition, the Holy Spirit spoke to me, and He said something that went very deep in my spirit: "I am going to make miracles in your move." This was an exciting time of transition, and we were looking for the Holy Spirit to breathe life onto our recent move.

While laying out in the sun thinking about the recent events leading up to this moment, I found myself mindful of the goodness of God. Taking in this moment of gratefulness, I could sense God's presence all around. The peace I was experiencing was oxygen to my soul. Lost in the moment, I was oblivious to everything around me and in a special place of connection to Jesus. It was then that my wife tapped me on the foot and brought me back to an awareness of my surroundings. She spoke my name as I came to. I felt like I was awakening from sleep.

"Jamie, get up. A four-year-old boy drowned."

"What?" I asked.

"I don't really know," she replied in a panic, "but there is a group of people trying to revive this boy on the other side of the pool."

I immediately got up and ran to see what was happening. Looking back, I could see my wife holding our four-year-old son in her arms and comforting our daughter. When I came to the area where they had the boy, the pool lifeguard was attempting CPR on him, trying to revive him the best he could. The mother was screaming and crying with the most desperate sound I have ever heard. People standing by were talking quietly about how the boy had been found by his five-year-old cousin floating at the bottom of the lazy river. The utter helplessness in the atmosphere was so thick; the only thing cutting through it was the sound of this mother crying for her child. I stood by with my father-in-law, praying in my spirit, "Do something, God. Please, do something."

Twenty minutes or so went by, and this boy still lay there unconscious and barely breathing. The CPR was not changing anything. Some were suggesting that the boy might have food stuck in his airway and were loudly encouraging the boy to throw up. Others were saying he possibly hit his head and fell unconscious into the pool. The resort paramedic was now trying to pump his lungs and remove any water he may have swallowed. Nothing was changing, and the boy was looking worse. His breathing was sporadic, and you could see this boy was fighting for his life.

It might have been 10 to 15 minutes later when the ambulance finally arrived. The EMT placed the boy on a stretcher and marched him off to the medical vehicle. The only sound you could hear in the whole resort was the sound of the mother wailing for her son's life. This four-year-old boy was now being hauled off in what felt like a funeral procession. People were trying to comfort the mother, but everyone there felt the darkness of what was happening to this family. I followed along, still praying, "Do something, God. Do something." I remember my thoughts as I tried to rationalize the situation: "At best, this boy is going to have severe brain damage," I thought.

As they rushed him into the ambulance, the mother still sobbing in despair, I continued to pray, "Do something, God. Do something." It was in that moment that I heard the Holy Spirit speak so clearly to my gut: "You do something." It was like something exploded in my spirit. I was determined to see this boy come back to us and fulfill his God-given destiny. My wife and I ran up to the mother, who was hysterical, and grabbed her hand. I could feel the desperation, and I spoke to her, "I am a healing minister. May I pray for your son?"

She yelled out, "Please, he is my only son!"

"What is his name?" I asked.

"Adam," She cried.

Emily, my wife, took one hand, and I took the other, and I spoke to the mother, "God is going to bring Adam back to us, and he is going to fulfill his destiny."

In that moment, I felt an intense shout rise out of my soul as I called out, "Adam, I speak to your spirit: Come back into your body! You will fulfill your destiny and do all that God has called you to do. You will live with full brain function and be healthy all the days of your life! God will watch over you, and you will see His goodness. Let the breath of God come into your lungs, in Jesus' name!" When my wife reached out to pray for Adam, she prayed from a deep place for life to come back into this boy as if she were praying for our own child. By now, many of those who had evacuated the pool area were gathering around this mother as my wife and I held on to her hands and interceded for the life of this boy. People who might not have prayed in years were praying. One man who did not know what to pray was uttering over and over, "Angels, angels, angels." Emily's father, Stephen, jumped in as well with a father's heart to see this mother's son come back to life.

Immediately, the EMT jumped out of the ambulance with news that the boy had awakened out of unconsciousness and was screaming with all the force his lungs could bear! The crowd participating and those watching had witnessed a miracle, and everyone knew it. The EMT reported that while they were attempting to put a medical device down the boy's throat, he woke up screaming. He was now fully alert and yelling out, "I don't want this!" about the device they were trying to use to bring him back to consciousness.

People were coming to the mother to celebrate what had just happened. Tears of joy were flowing down her face. Everyone standing by the scene was stunned, and the awe of God permeated the atmosphere. I stood by and watched people say the name of Jesus like they were saying it for the first time in many years as they recognized the miracle of life Jesus had given this boy. Emily and I were hugging Adam's mother and blessing God's incredible salvation.

A holy hush then set in as my wife and I made our way back to our car. The parking lot for the resort pool was a small walk to the other side of the road. Holding my son in my arms and holding my daughter's hand, I spoke to my wife without words. Our immense gratefulness for what God had just done was now pouring into our family. We were in awe. While we strapped our kids in, my wife and I kept making eye contact with each other and shaking our heads in astonishment.

I went around to the front door of the driver's side and looked up to find a man standing still beside a white van, staring at me. I had not seen this man before, but he looked at me and spoke my name like he knew me.

"Jamie," he said.

"Yes?" I replied.

"Is the boy okay?"

"Yes," I answered.

Now getting in his white van, he spoke with an unusual sense of calm. "Good," he said.

After he drove away, I looked over at Emily in shock. We stared at each other stunned, trying to make sense of it all. "That was very strange. How did that man know my name?" I said to Emily.

"I don't know what's going on here, but I think that may have been an angel."

The Scripture tells us, *"Do not neglect to show hospitality to strangers, for by this some have entertained angels without knowing it"* (Heb. 13:2 NASB). If this man was an angel, I would be the one within this verse not "knowing it." And if God did send His angel, it was to watch over the miracle of life that Jesus had done for this little boy.

"What happened to the boy?" you ask. As we drove away, we could see the helicopter airlifting him to the nearest major hospital. He was being rushed there to see if any brain damage had occurred during his time of unconsciousness. A couple days later, Emily was walking around the resort and recognized one of the faces of the family. It was the boy's uncle, and he was taking a group of kids out for some fun. My wife introduced herself and asked about the boy. The uncle responded with incredible news: Adam was just fine, healthy, and not a single bit of brain damage was found! Not only that, but he wanted to go back to the pool! My wife was shocked. The boy's uncle continued to tell her that Adam could not recall the incident; his only memory was that he had been in a special place where he could breathe underwater. I believe Adam was in the Spirit with the presence of God.

It is moments like this—otherworldly moments—that have captured my attention. There is another reality where angels, miracles, and the supernatural are being orchestrated by the Lord of Hosts to bring the Kingdom of Heaven to earth and to reveal the goodness of God. This invisible world is actively hidden right in front of our eyes. Every day there are supernatural moments that are so covert they might be missed unless we have eyes to see them.

Personally, I am curious and want to know more. I want to see the invisible activities of Heaven. Are there ways to peer into these hidden realities? Can we recognize both the obvious actions and the subtleties of God? I believe so, and it is a passion of mine to discover the ways of God and to see past the realm of the natural into the realm of the supernatural. Perhaps God is looking for those who will try to find what He is hiding in plain sight!

It is the glory of God to conceal a matter, but the glory of kings is to search out a matter (Proverbs 25:2).

MADE YOU LOOK

But why don't more people experience this unseen reality? If it is that powerful—enough to influence the world in which we live—why is it not taught in schools or referenced in common conversation? If we can see its influence, why is it sort of looked down upon in some social and church circles to talk about it? I think it all comes down to this one thing: Are people looking and paying attention to it, or are we trained to ignore what is right in front of our noses?

When I was a kid, I played a game called "made you look." In the game, we would make the person look at something by pointing

14

out something passing by. This was often a game that we would play on long road trips in the car to keep us amused. We would say something like, "Look at that tree over there!" The other person would quickly turn their head and look. At that point, we would say, "Made you look!" No matter how many times we did this, it always seemed fun and new. "Made you look" became one of our favorite games on the road. The things that we would make someone look at were always there. The difference is, they normally weren't paying enough attention to focus and look at them. There is an unseen world right in front of our eyes. We may not see it because we do not look.

While we do not look at the things which are seen, but at the things which are not seen. For the things which are seen are temporary, but the things which are not seen are eternal (2 Corinthians 4:18).

When we focus in on something, we begin to connect with it. There is a difference between seeing and looking. Seeing happens to a person; looking is the action the individual takes even before they see it. In this book, I want to help you know what to look for! Everyone has the eyes to see, but not all look. What are we looking for? We're looking for things that are not seen! Things around us are temporary. Temporary things fade away, but the Kingdom of God lasts forever. Imagine a world where color is so much brighter—a bustling world full of movement and daily activity. In the created world, we are all being impacted and influenced by a culture outside of the natural realm. When we live in the natural world without this knowledge, we do not consider the effect that the invisible realm has on our visible day.

What if I told you that there was another reality that has a direct impact on the world in which you live? What if I told you that this world, this reality, could not help but be influenced by a coinciding alternate reality? Now by "alternate" I do not mean the opposite. This alternate reality directly occurs simultaneously with the world that we live in right now. If I told you that there were invisible advantages you could access at any given moment, would you want to know about them? Of course you would! But what if I told you that there are invisible disadvantages being played out in your life? Some of these disadvantages you might be aware of, and some of them you may not. These disadvantages may play against you in everyday situations. But what are these advantages and disadvantages?

DIVINE APPOINTMENT

The truth is, the number of invisible realities in a normal day would totally blow us away. We may not realize it, but an average day has hidden and invisible mechanics happening at every turn. Getting to work on time, getting delayed, a chance meeting with that certain someone, the dog pulling you in a new direction—these events may seem all too normal, but there are very few, if any, random happenings in our day. Each and every day, a divine selection of events occurs, appointments and disappointments that change the course of history in our life one moment at a time. *The Merriam-Webster Learner's Dictionary* defines appointment as:

> an agreement to meet with someone at a particular time
> the act of giving a particular job or position to someone:
> the act of appointing someone a job or duty that is given
> to a person: a position to which someone is appointed.[1]

An appointment is a convergence of two or more things at a particular place and time. When these things come together, we experience an appointment. When God sets something up and we meet someone or find something somewhere, we have what I call a "divine appointment"—a moment appointed by the Spirit of God where destiny meets reality and invisible worlds become visible. In this convergence of life, we experience a moment with God, but we may not realize it. We may have been led to think this is luck, but what if it is something more? And if there is something more going on, can I as a believer become more intentional about noticing these moments? Is it even possible to step into these moments more often?

There are invisible problems happening around us as well. While God is constantly setting up divine appointments, we can also experience what the enemy is trying to set up. The enemy wants to dis-appoint us from our divine appointment. *The Merriam-Webster Learner's Dictionary* defines disappointment as:

> the state of feeling of being disappointed someone or something that disappoints people: a disappointing person or thing.[2]

The enemy is constantly trying to dismantle our divine appointment. God means for good and the enemy for evil. So now we are faced with an invisible reality. What do I do about this? What can I do about this? The normal life in Jesus is designed to be an increasing string of divine appointments. The secret to a life filled with divine appointments is hidden in plain sight. When we understand this secret, it's a game changer!

THE SECRET THINGS

The secret things belong to the Lord our God, but those things which are revealed belong to us and to our children forever, that we may do all the words of this law (Deuteronomy 29:29).

Have you ever met someone who has a really difficult time keeping secrets? Maybe you know someone who seems to be overly excited to tell you something secret. There are certain things that God keeps secret, but then there are other things that He loves to reveal. Secrets are the wonder of God. He may not be the author of confusion, but make no mistake—He is a God of mystery and secrecy. God knows things, and He knows what we do not know. He takes those things that we do not know and prepares them for a great reveal. In doing so, He invites us into a mysterious encounter with His secrets.

We may think of property as something material someone has in their possession. It could be a house, a piece of land, a car, or a boat. While material possessions can be passed down from one generation to another, so can spiritual secrets. Consider it like intellectual property, which *The Merriam-Webster Dictionary* defines as:

> property (such as an idea, invention, or process) that derives from the work of the mind or intellect; *also* : an application, right, or registration relating to this.[3]

The things that are revealed were once hidden things. These things may have been there the whole time, hidden in plain sight, but once they are revealed they belong to those to whom they have been entrusted. Like the passing of property from one generation to another, God is raising up a generation to which He can reveal His mysteries. This generation will be called to steward the greatest secrets of all time. What mysteries and wonders wait for those who are willing to go beyond the veil and peer past the seen into the unseen? Where are those whom God can trust with these secrets? Who are they, and what do they look like?

THE ORIGINAL MAN

In the beginning, God formed paradise by His word. Creation came together to form the most beautiful display of life on planet Earth. Within a matter of moments, out of nothing came something. Genesis, the book of beginnings, tells us that God set this garden in the East and it is there that *"He put the man whom He had formed"* (Gen. 2:8). In the Garden, God brought Adam through an unusual task:

> *Out of the ground the Lord God formed every beast of the field and every bird of the air, and brought them to Adam to see what he would call them. And whatever Adam called each living creature, that was its name* (Genesis 2:19).

This was a job that would require a grace that was beyond natural skill or talent. Adam was called on to name each and every living thing. The lion, the bear, the bird—everything that crawls, flies, swims, etc., would be named by Adam. This was no easy task, and Adam was not simply naming categories of animals. Adam was called on by God to name every living thing and every variation of that living thing. Think about the length and difficulty of this task. With the thousands of species of birds and the vast varieties of big animals, rodents, wild cats, and every other type of living creature, this was no small feat. Adam answered the call and named every created thing. With what secret genius was Adam operating? The secret is found within Genesis, hidden in plain sight. Buried within the words of the scriptural account we find the key: *"the Lord God...brought them to Adam to see"* (Gen. 2:19). The word translated as "to see" that describes the event of Adam seeing the animals is the Hebrew word *ra'ah*. This word can become lost in translation as a simple verb, "to see," but Adam was seeing deeper than the natural eye typically does.

We have to understand that Adam walked with God and saw the Father. In the cool of the Garden, the Father would walk with Adam. At the Fall of Adam and Eve, the Father is caught walking in the cool of the day, crying out for His creation:

> *And they heard the sound of the Lord God walking in the garden in the cool of the day, and Adam and his wife hid themselves from the presence of the Lord God among the trees of the garden. Then the Lord God called to Adam and said to him, "Where are you?"* (Genesis 3:8-9)

Adam and Eve had the ability to see the invisible God! Perhaps Adam's sight was not the same as most of us are used to. I venture to say that Adam was able to see the invisible nature of every living thing. As he pronounced the name of each creature, he was articulating his perception of its invisible qualities. Adam could penetrate into the depths of what many simply observe superficially. This distinct quality gave him the unique ability to name the animal kingdom. He could see to the core of the creation and perceive what each creature was made to become!

I know some of you reading this might have imagined at some point in your childhood what it would be like to see through walls. Adam had something far greater. He could see the invisible nature of the world around him. That instinct is the unseen essence of something known only to Creator God. But when God invited Adam to see the animals, he saw them with the same perspective with which God sees.

THE SEER'S HOUSE

rō'eh

By the time Israel was being established by God as a great nation, something unique was taking place. Seers were becoming an integral part of society.

Formerly in Israel, if someone went to inquire of God, they would say, *"Come, let us go to the seer,"* because the prophet of today used to be called a seer (see 1 Sam. 9:9).

Seers shared things with the people of the day. Perhaps they shared the mysteries of God! We do know for sure that they shared the secrets of what the future held. It seemed to be customary that when visiting the seer, one would bring some food as a sort of offering (see 1 Sam. 9:7). The locals knew about the seer, as evidenced by the fact that the soon-to-be king, Saul, asks some of the locals on his journey, *"Is the seer here?"* (1 Sam. 9:11). They seem to casually respond about his whereabouts, sending Saul on his way to meet the seer. Saul stumbles into a divine appointment with the one he is looking for and asks him, *"Please tell me, where is the seer's house?"* (1 Sam. 9:18). Then *"Samuel answered Saul and said, 'I am the seer. Go up before me to the high place, for you shall eat with me today; and tomorrow I will let you go and will tell you all that is in your heart'"* (1 Sam. 9:19).

Seer
Verb: Hebrew. רָאָה *ra'ah*
: to see, perceive, have vision.[4]

Samuel was a seer of the highest accuracy. He could tell you the secrets of your heart, the things that no one else knew. His sight was beyond the natural into the invisible realities of the heart. Just as Adam could see the invisible qualities of each animal, Samuel the seer had vision to see what no one else did.

Saul did not realize it that day, but his chance encounter with the seer was a divine appointment. Heaven was inviting him to the seer's house to hear the secrets only Heaven knew. This same invitation comes to us today. God invites us to see the world around us with a different set of eyes. With this in mind, I invite you into *Secrets of the Seer*.

SECRETS OF THE SEER

I have made it a personal mission to discover the secret things of God. What I have found is that not only are there secrets that God is keeping, but it seems that there are secret ways to discover the secrets God is desiring to speak. *Secrets of the Seer* is a compilation of practices and perspectives that I have found increase the frequency of seer encounters in my life. Some of these secrets are ancient biblical practices, while others are ancient biblical knowledge. Each of them, when observed, takes us into a place of encounter that seers of old would consider sacred.

> *And it shall come to pass in the last days, says God, that I will pour out of My Spirit on all flesh; your sons and your daughters shall prophesy, your young men shall see visions, your old men shall dream dreams. And on My menservants and on My maidservants I will pour out My Spirit in those days; and they shall prophesy* (Acts 2:17-18).

In the last days, there will be an unprecedented level of dreams and visions. Young and old will experience supernatural seer phenomena, and the world will witness a global outpouring, where people from every nation, tribe, and culture will be wondering about the encounters they are having in their sleep and the visions they are having during the day. Before this time comes, a company of seers and prophetic voices will emerge with the ability to help people understand the mystery of these events in their lives. Imagine a community of seers who are able to tell the world the meaning of these dreams and encounters. Much like Joseph with Pharaoh or Daniel with Nebuchadnezzar, there will come a time when world leaders will search the globe for someone with answers to the mystery of the encounters they are having. Dreamers will look for understanding

22

of their dreams or the supernatural lights that keep visiting them at night. Others will be like Cornelius, who had an encounter with an angel while praying and was told to look for a man named Peter. The angel's final instruction to Cornelius about Peter was, *"He will tell you what you must do"* (Acts 10:6). Encounters like this will be something we can expect, and at that time a great company of seers and prophets will emerge with the wisdom and know-how to interpret these moments for the people looking for answers. These are times of supernatural moments, where mature seers will need to be readily available because the world stage will be set for their involvement.

I am writing this with the intention to prepare the way for a generation of highly skilled and fully engaged seers and prophets who practice a lifestyle of pursuing God's presence with eyes to see, ears to hear, and hearts that are entirely committed to understanding the wonder of God's ways. When these perspectives and practices are observed, I believe it will create an environment within our own life that will enable us to experience seer moments that reveal Heaven's activity all around us.

CHAPTER 2

THE SECRET OF
HEAVEN ON EARTH

Praise be to the God and Father of our Lord Jesus Christ, who has blessed us in the heavenly realms with every spiritual blessing in Christ.

—EPHESIANS 1:3 NIV

Ten geographers who think the world is flat will tend to reinforce each other's errors.... Only a sailor can set them straight.

—JOHN RALSTON SAUL

The Greek philosopher Aristotle had a unique observation about the spherical shape of the earth. The circular shadow cast on the moon during a lunar eclipse gave him insight into this.[5] While this might seem like a common-sense understanding of the earth, the Flat Earth Society would disagree. Some would even go so far as to argue that all space travel accomplishments are nothing more than a conspiracy orchestrated by NASA. They would deny the existence of a "flat earth conspiracy" and assert that it should more likely be called a "space travel conspiracy."[6]

Our understanding of the universe is expanding. NASA continues to make discoveries beyond our solar system and now, with the introduction of quantum physics, we are studying not only the expanding universe, but the nature of atoms and subatomic particles as well. What lies next in our field of discovery? While historically science and spirituality have often clashed, the future is open for change.

Among other things, human consciousness has become a subject of debate. The subject at hand: How are physical actions shaped by nonphysical thoughts? Is there another world shaping our consciousness, or does the physical world shape our consciousness? What is consciousness, and how is it formed?

The incredible world as we know it is filled with layers of coinciding realities. Within each of these realities exist patterns and recognizable differences. For instance, fire is the cause of destruction on earth, but it may have different properties in Heaven. In Revelation 15:2, we find a special group of overcomers standing on what appears to be *a sea of glass mingled with fire.* Whether the fire is different or our ability to handle fire will be different in Heaven is to be discovered. What is evident is that there are two very different effects that fire can have on you depending on where you are at! While I would never personally recommend standing on fire here on earth, it seems to be a glorious honor in Heaven.

Let's look at the moment when Adam and Eve discover that they are naked. We are told that *"they were both naked, the man and his wife, and were not ashamed"* (Gen. 2:25). Their nakedness was not a big deal to them; in fact, it was not even something they realized. When they were naked, they walked around free, without shame, but something changed. When they ate the fruit from the tree of knowledge of good and evil, they stepped out of one awareness and into another type of awareness.

> *Then the eyes of both of them were opened, and they knew that they were naked; and they sewed fig leaves together and made themselves coverings* (Genesis 3:7).

Their eyes were opened? How could their eyes be opened when Adam saw the animals and named them? How did Adam and Eve see the world before the Fall? God asks Adam, *"Who told you that you were naked?" (Gen. 3:11).* They had been naked the entire time, but now they see? How could Adam see the animals but not his own nakedness? The question is, if Adam and Eve originally were naked and not ashamed, only to realize after the Fall that they were naked and in need of clothes, what kept them from seeing their own nakedness? Perhaps they were living clothed in a different reality beyond the one we understand as normal to us. I believe that Adam and Eve lived with eyes wide open to a reality much higher than ours. They saw the glory of God, the full revelation of the Father. They did not look at things the way we see them. When they looked at each other before the Fall, they did not see nakedness. They knew each other by the glory that surrounded them. The glory of God was the lens through which they looked. The glory of God was their covering, and this covering acted like God goggles. When the glory lifted, they saw the simplicity of man without it—naked and needing clothing. God's desire in Christ is *"bringing many sons and daughters to glory"* (Heb. 2:10 NIV). God is bringing us back to the place where we can live here, present with the world around us yet looking at life through the lens of the glory of God.

BILOCATIONAL

Jesus spoke something incredible to Nicodemus. His great reveal to the spiritual leader of the day, Nicodemus, in John 3 contains something often overlooked, but if you slow down your reading of the passage it shows us that something more than meets the eye is happening with Jesus.

> *No one has ascended to heaven but He who came down from heaven, that is, the Son of Man who is in heaven* (John 3:13).

Hidden in plain sight, Jesus reveals to Nicodemus that He is in Heaven at that current moment: *"the Son of Man who is in heaven"* (John 3:13).

What is wild to me is Jesus is communicating to Nicodemus not only where He is from, but also where He is at the same time. Nicodemus was attempting to solve a riddle. The big question in his heart: Where was Jesus from?

> *Rabbi, we know that You are a teacher come from God; for no one can do these signs that You do unless God is with him. Jesus answered and said to him, "Most assuredly, I say to you, unless one is born again, he cannot see the kingdom of God." Nicodemus said to Him, "How can a man be born when he is old? Can he enter a second time into his mother's womb and be born?" Jesus answered, "Most assuredly, I say to you,*

unless one is born of water and the Spirit, he cannot enter the kingdom of God. That which is born of the flesh is flesh, and that which is born of the Spirit is spirit. Do not marvel that I said to you, 'You must be born again'" (John 3:2-5).

For many years, I grew up hearing this passage as a formulaic method to ensure I go to Heaven when I die. "You must be born again to go to Heaven when you die!" the preacher would say. The odd thing is in John 3, the word die or death is not mentioned once. If death is not the issue at hand, what is the conversation between Jesus and Nicodemus about? Nicodemus had a burning question: Where is Jesus from, and how is He doing these miracles?

What if I told you the original man was created to live in two places at one time—that God made Adam and Eve to walk with Him in the cool of the Garden of Eden and at the same time have access to Him in heavenly places? What if I told you that as a new creation in Christ, you are in two places at one time as well?

*If then **you were raised with Christ**, seek those things which are above, **where Christ is, sitting at the right hand of God**. Set your mind on things above, not on things on the earth. For you died, and **your life is hidden with Christ in God**. When Christ who is our life appears, then you also will appear with Him in glory* (Colossians 3:1-4).

While you and I are on this earth as a vessel for God to work through, the other half of that same coin is that we have been raised with Christ to sit at the right hand of God. He *"raised us up together, and made us sit together in the heavenly places in Christ Jesus"* (Eph. 2:6). What is interesting here is that Jesus modeled something every believer can live out. He was bilocational.

bilocation

noun bi·lo·ca·tion \'bī-lō-ˌkā-shən\
: the state of being or ability to be
in two places at the same time[7]

Jesus lived out a life on earth, fully human, and yet was able to do miracles as if He was from a different planet. It made Nicodemus question everything and humbled him to the point of seeking out the most controversial voice in his time. When he comes to Jesus, he wants to know, "What is the secret?" Jesus reveals to him one of the greatest secrets of all time—**the secret of Heaven on earth.**

The secret of Heaven on earth is the mystery behind Jesus' ability to manifest the miraculous. He was here and there at the same time. Unfortunately, the power behind this secret has been lost and replaced with the traditional view that Heaven is a place you go to only when you die. If that is the sole reality of Heaven, then it would not be a place for the living but for the dead. Yet Jesus challenges this notion by describing the nature of God as follows: *"He is not the God of the dead, but the God of the living"* (Mark 12:27). The enemy hates this secret and wants to make it something reachable only by death. Why? The enemy hates Heaven. He used to live there and was kicked out. Since being kicked out, he now despises anything to do with Heaven. He has now hijacked the theology of Heaven and has hidden its power in the life of the believer here on earth.

CONVERGENCE

Seers walk in heavenly realities here on earth. Jesus was the ultimate seer in that He demonstrated the convergence between Heaven and earth. Whenever Heaven and earth come together, that is the convergence of two realities in one space. What happens in convergence is what we call a miracle—two dimensions coming together in one space to reveal the glory of God. Seers live in that space. They have one eye in the natural and another in the supernatural. The main writer of the New Testament has this to say about life on earth:

> *I have been crucified with Christ; it is no longer I who live, but Christ lives in me; and the life which I now live in the flesh I live by faith in the Son of God, who loved me and gave Himself for me* (Galatians 2:20).

What I find interesting here is that Paul mentions how he is living in his flesh by faith. This might contradict the popular teaching that the flesh is evil and that God wants nothing to do with the flesh. That kind of teaching has put a kill switch on the glory of God in man. And if the flesh is evil, how is it that Jesus came in the flesh?

> *And without controversy great is the mystery of godliness: God was manifested in the flesh, justified in the Spirit, seen by angels, preached among the Gentiles, believed on in the world, received up in glory* (1 Timothy 3:16).

The convergence of flesh and spirit brought the Son of God into this world. And if flesh is evil, how is it that Paul the apostle possibly went to Heaven in the body?

> *I must go on boasting. Although there is nothing to be gained, I will go on to visions and revelations from the Lord. I know a man in Christ who fourteen years ago was caught up to the third heaven. Whether it was in the body or out of the body I do not know—God knows. And I know that this man—whether in the body or apart from the body I do not know, but God knows—was caught up to paradise and heard inexpressible things, things that no one is permitted to tell* (2 Corinthians 12:1-4 NIV).

There are encounters with Heaven that God has reserved for this generation that will mirror Paul's own wonder. Some will be caught up to the third heaven and wonder if it is possible it was in the body. We hear stories of near-death experiences where some talk about seeing Heaven after flatlining on the operating table. Paul's report is that he went to Heaven even before death. He even mentioned the possibility that he went there in the body, not out of the body like we hear in these near-death experiences. And if the body is not evil but has been made righteous through the cross of Jesus, it certainly is possible.

PARALLEL UNIVERSE

When Heaven and earth touch, something shifts, and one reality begins to shape and influence the other. The universe is out of alignment. Much like a chiropractor bringing adjustment to a misaligned spine, the Holy Spirit is orchestrating all things to come back into alignment with Jesus. What happens in alignment is that we begin to see parallel encounters. If the world is multidimensional, there are things that are happening in the multiple realities that echo one another. When these alignments begin to occur, things around us shift into place to usher in a move of God. This, in very simple terms, is earth coming into alignment with Heaven.

This became clear to me years ago when my wife and I had our first child. We were in the middle of a season of shift where we felt God was leading us in a different direction. We did not know where we were going, but we felt the stirring inside our heart that a new assignment was coming up. We were part of a great missionary organization at the time, leading and directing the prophetic ministry, but we could feel the shift.

One morning I was speaking at a local house group in eastern Pennsylvania. A handful of people gathered, getting ready to worship, and I was brought in to minister the message that morning. Before the message, I was lying down, getting ready for the meeting. The meeting was about to start in one hour, and I found a quiet place to rest and ask Holy Spirit what He wanted to do that morning. It was totally unexpected, but as I lay down to wait for the Father's voice, I went into an encounter. An angel appeared to me. It had a similar appearance to my wife, and it was pregnant. When I looked at the angel, I had an immediate download. It was as if we were speaking without words. The messenger angel revealed to me in that moment that my wife was pregnant and that it was a sign to me that the region we were in was pregnant as well. I was stunned. When I came out of the encounter, I immediately called my wife. I told her, "You are pregnant!" She was stunned too and did not know what to do with the revelation. We bought two tests from a local dollar store to see if she was pregnant or not. Each one came back with such a faint sign that we could not tell if it was a plus or a minus. Mystified, I was now sent out on a journey to the local pharmacy to find the most elaborate pregnancy test possible. We were determined. The one I found was so clear, it would be impossible for us to screw it up! She took the test, and it showed what looked like a division sign (/). Wait, what? What is this? So, we scheduled a doctor visit because we were still unclear about the tests' results. When we walked into the doctor appointment, we had anticipation in our hearts. The doctor put the instrument to my wife's belly, and we heard the angelic sound of our daughter's heartbeat for the first time. We sat there weeping over God's goodness.

It became apparent that God was trying to get our attention. While we sat there stunned at His love for our family, we began to have a deep realization that the region to which we would be called in that next season would be eastern Pennsylvania. It was not a small sign to us that the angel was communicating with me about the region being pregnant, just as my wife was pregnant. It would be the word from which we would pioneer for the next six years of our lives.

The convergence of parallel realities began to make sense. There was a sign in the spirit with the angel revealing my wife's pregnancy, a sign in the natural with my wife being pregnant, and a sign for the purposes of God to be released over a region. It is moments like this that are the convergence of multiple layers that demonstrate where Heaven is touching earth!

KEYS TO UNLOCKING THIS SECRET

The question to begin asking is, what is Heaven doing in my life right now? How can I identify it—seeing it in the spirit, reflected in the natural? Here are some practical steps to accessing the secret of Heaven on earth:

Start off in the natural world.

Observe the themes taking place. The Scripture gives a principle that the natural is first and then the spiritual: *"However, the spiritual is not first, but the natural, and afterward the spiritual"* (1 Cor. 15:46).

There will be naturally occurring phenomena in your life that are more spiritual than we realize. This is why babies in scriptural history were often named according to the times and happenings of the day. An example of this is Peleg. *"To Eber were born two sons: the name of one was Peleg, for in his days the earth was divided; and his brother's name was Joktan"* (Gen. 10:25). Peleg means "split or divide," so his parents named him according to an event.

Watch the clock.

God works in times and seasons. Often, a set of numbers will stand out to me. I don't go hunting for these numbers, but they will be numbers that accord with something seemingly heavenly happening at that time. If I wake up at 3:33 A.M. several nights in a row from a great dream, I should know that God is speaking about a convergence. It is a time that Heaven is touching down in the space I am in. What do I do with those numbers? I often go straight to Scripture to find their meaning or even to locate a parallel verse with the numbers in them. Wisdom tells us, *"In all your ways acknowledge Him, and He shall direct your paths"* (Prov. 3:6). As we acknowledge Him in everything, we see we are looking for evidence of Heaven touching earth.

CHAPTER
3

THE SECRET OF
ENTERTAINING ANGELS

Bless the Lord, all you His hosts, You ministers of His, who do His pleasure.

—Psalm 103:21

I then turned and saw that the entire army of the Lord was standing in that garden. There were men, women and children from all races and nations, each carrying their banners, which moved in the wind with perfect unity. I knew that nothing like this had been seen on the earth before. Although the enemy had many more armies and fortresses throughout the earth, I knew that none could stand before this great army of God.

Almost under my breath, I said, "This must be the day of the Lord." To my amazement, the whole host then answered in an awesome thunder, "The day of the Lord of Hosts has come!"

—Rick Joyner, *The Vision*

On a ski trip around the age of eight, my father took me up on a high slope at a Colorado ski resort. My father was an avid lover of skiing and wanted us to learn skiing at an early age. Now if you know something about skiing, you know that there are several levels of difficulties of slopes ranging from beginner, to skilled, to thrill-seeking, death-defying action hero. My father started me off on an easy slope, suited me up in a brand-new winter coat, slapped some skis on me, and sent me off on my way. It seemed easy enough, so the next day my Pops increased the challenge. He told me he wanted to get me on a black diamond run that day. I asked what that was, and he said, "It is the second most difficult slope there is on that ski resort." Braving it, I was up for the challenge!

It started off really well. It was a steep gradient of at least 40 percent, which means that it was *straight down*. About 30 seconds into the run I fell flat on my back. The only problem was my skis were still on the icy snow beneath me! I kept trying to get up, but I could not. My skis were stuck and so was I. Lying on my back, I slid straight down this slope like a little snow coat torpedo. My father said it all happened so fast. He couldn't catch up with me, and no one really could. I must have picked up some miles per hour that were faster than a normal person could ski on this black diamond because no one was coming to my rescue. My dad said that out of nowhere a mystery skier flew down the trail like it was nothing. I was heading straight for a line of trees at a speed that definitely would have hospitalized me. My father was helplessly yelling something at me when I felt arms pick me up, set me on my feet, pat my head, and ski off into the distance. My father sat there stunned and could not put together who this mystery person was. He was skiing too fast to be a normal or even expert skier. He was convinced it was an angel! When we got back to the lodge, my new winter coat had a permanent stripe down the back of it where the ice had stripped off the dye on the coat. I have no idea how fast I was going, but it was fast enough to strip the color off a brand-new winter coat!

Angels have been saving lives since the beginning of history. Lot was saved by a company of angels who assisted his family's exodus out of Sodom at the right time (see Gen. 19). It was an angel who shut the mouth of the lions and kept Daniel from being eaten in the lion's den (see Dan. 6:22). It was an angel who rescued Peter from prison, *"saying, 'Arise quickly!' And his chains fell of his hands"* (Acts 12:7b).

It's no secret that angels are real, but many of us have had angelic encounters without even knowing it. *"Do not neglect to show hospitality to strangers, for by this some have entertained angels without knowing it"* (Heb. 13:2 NASB). They seem to be messengers who show themselves without seeking glory so as to go out of the way to make you know they are an angel. The seer has another secret; it is **the secret of entertaining angels.**

Angels are not as distant as we may think. They are not sent to us only in certain dire moments of distress, although they do seem to be more pronounced when emergency moments are happening. I often believe this is because we are desperate enough to be open for help when most of the time we need help but are just too hesitant to admit it. The secret of entertaining angels is the beautiful mystery of the interaction between God's created order. Entertaining angels is far different than worshiping angels. The worship of angels is forbidden and unnecessary, and while angels are glorious in their strength, they do not appreciate worship directed toward them. In fact, John the beloved, while receiving the Revelation of Jesus Christ, writes that while being escorted by an angel in heavenly encounter, he fell down to worship the angel for all the things that were shown to him, and the angel responded, *"See that you do not do that. For I am your fellow servant, and of your brethren the prophets, and of those who keep the words of this book. Worship God"* (Rev. 22:9).

RELEASE OF HEAVENLY BEINGS

We tend to give everything we experience from God or the devil an easy identifier so that we can label what we see as either good or evil. If it is good, it was God, and if we are really spiritual, we might call it angel. There has been a wonderful introduction of angels to the Body of Christ over the last several decades. We are now becoming more familiar and comfortable with language that describes angelic activity. I believe angelic activity will increase until the coming of Jesus. The Revelation describes angelic activity in the last days with a heightened frequency. It even reveals that an angel will be sent to preach the Gospel. *"Then I saw another angel flying in the midst of heaven, having the everlasting gospel to preach to those who dwell on the earth—to every nation, tribe, tongue, and people"* (Rev. 14:6). Record numbers of people are coming to the goodness of salvation in Jesus each and every day. What's more amazing is that many of them are being led to Jesus through angelic ministry. I have spoken to people in the Middle East, and their testimonies indicate that angelic sightings seem to be an experience some have in coming to know Jesus as Messiah. With all these sightings and angelic interventions, the Spirit of God wants us to be in the know and help us understand the secret of entertaining angels.

What constitutes a host, and what or who are angels? Each and every one of us can be familiar with this secret. We are surrounded by angels on every side (see Ps. 34:7). With this in mind, we can get to know the mysteries of angelic ministry and the hosts of Heaven.

PARTNERING WITH ANGELS

The Lord has established His throne in heaven, and His kingdom rules over all. Bless the Lord, you His angels, who excel in strength, who do His word, heeding the voice of His word. Bless the Lord, all you His hosts, you ministers of His, who do His pleasure. Bless the Lord, all His works, in all places of His dominion. Bless the Lord, O my soul! (Psalm 103:19-22)

"Why angels?" some might ask. "Why not Jesus doing it, or Holy Spirit?" To clearly understand this, we must appreciate the glory of our King. Jesus is a King. He is not a servant, though He came as one, but Father, Son, and Holy Spirit are the triune God. To ask God to do all the work Himself is like asking a king to mow the lawn in front of his castle himself. Too often we forget that God is King, and a King has servants. Each servant has a role, each role has a purpose, and every purpose makes the Kingdom move forward until it takes over every sphere of influence.

As we look at the order of the heavens we see that the Father *"has established His throne in heaven, and His kingdom rules over all"* (Ps. 103:19). The Kingdom of God is designed to expand. Jesus compared it to leaven: *"The kingdom of heaven is like leaven, which a woman took and hid in three measure of meal till it was all leavened"* (Matt. 13:33). When the Kingdom of God expands, the dominion of His rule and rein increases. That means the enemies of the Kingdom weaken and decrease. What are the enemies? Jesus named the enemies that He was after: sickness, broken-heartedness, poverty, oppression, slavery, etc. (see Luke 4:18-19). So, how can we partner with Jesus to expand His Kingdom? Understanding angels and hosts gives us clear insight into stewarding this secret.

Angels, it reads, *"do His word, heeding the voice of His word"* (Ps. 103:20). What is the difference between His word and the voice of His word? His word is what He speaks, and the voice of His word is the word He speaks through us! God is speaking, and the angels are listening. They are listening to God, waiting for His command. The other odd thing that I have witnessed in the spirit is that angels are also waiting for the words that are God's words coming out of our mouths. Jesus said, *"by the mouth of two or three witnesses every word may be established"* (Matt. 18:16). As words are established in agreement, the angels of God hear it as though the word from the Holy Spirit was whispered in our hearts and spoken out loud where they are able to hear it for the first time. They hear it, discerning that it sounds like something God would say, and act on it, trusting that the Father has spoken clearly to us and we have clearly heard Him. This partnership between the Father and the angels sets a new precedent for us as sons and daughters. Will we speak His word, knowing that it puts angelic help in motion?

There was a moment in ministry where a young man had just received Jesus. We were on the street corner, and he came to Christ. It was beautiful. With his eyes closed, he asked Jesus to come into his life that day. I asked him to open his eyes, and when he did, I asked if the world seemed brighter with Jesus now in his heart. Looking around, he responded with a surprising, "Not really." I was shocked and asked, puzzled, "Why not?" He then said, "I am color blind." As soon as he said that, I blurted out, "God is going to heal you!" The angels must have heard that because what happened next amazed me. I asked the Holy Spirit to send an angel to put his hand on his head. Much to my amazement, the young man responded, "There is a hand on my head!" I then asked the Holy Spirit to have that angel put his hand through his head and touch his eyes. Startled, he told me, "There is a hand in my head touching my eyes!" In that moment, he opened his eyes again and he could see in color for the first time in his life! It was a miracle. We both stood there in awe at the grace of God.

A week later, I was at the street corner directly across from where we were before. I found myself in a casual conversation about God with another man. As we were talking, I kept being unusually drawn to his eyes. It wouldn't go away so I finally asked if there was anything different about his eyes. It was sort of a strange question from a stranger on the street, but God works in mysterious ways! He told me, "I don't know what you mean. Well, I am, uh, color blind." When he said "color blind," it was like lightning shot through me, and I blurted out again, "God is going to heal you!" Once again—and I am not sure if it was the same angel—I prayed, just like I did the week before! "There is a hand in my head touching my eyes!" he told me. It was an angel of God healing this man of his color blindness, just like the one who was healed the week before. That man came to a local gathering we had planned for the next night. We started talking, and he opened the conversation by telling me how he is having a hard time wrapping his mind around the fact that he had been healed! It was so beautiful how Jesus did it.

FLASHES OF LIGHT

Something began happening to me when my eyes were opened to see in the spirit. Flashes of light would appear out of the corner of my eye, and it seemed as if they would disappear when I turned to look at them. This made me wonder what was happening. Perhaps I was having eye problems. The colors of the flashes were not all the same, though, which made me more curious. Sometimes it would be a blue flash of light and at other times a gold flash. It stayed long enough for me to notice but not long enough for me to study. I could not wrap my mind around what was happening. I began to ask the Father for revelation. I remember going to bed one night and having a dream about these lights. In the dream, I saw a ball of energy filled with the life-giving healing presence of Heaven. There was electricity around these orb-looking beings. I was shown in the dream that when I felt heat when ministering, it was a host bringing healing, and when I felt electricity, it was a host bringing a miracle.

I noticed after this dream that when I prayed for people for healing, many would report a sensation of heat on their body where the pain was. When the heat stayed for a while, the pain left. I also noticed when I prayed for someone needing a miracle, I would feel an electric-like sensation on my hand. I was experiencing the dream! Were these the hosts I had seen in my dream at night? I began to reach out to God for more on the hosts. If there were mysteries, I was curious and wanted to discover more! What were the hosts, and how could I further partner with Heaven to see their release?

The hosts are described as *"ministers of His, who do His pleasure"* (Ps. 103:21). The word minister here is similar to a butler. Some might call them the butlers of God. They are there as hosts, hosting God's presence in whatever makes the King happy to do. And similar to the way someone can be a host of something contagious, hosts are hosting grace from the presence of God that is imparted to those needing a fresh touch of God's presence. The wild thing is, when a host from Heaven comes, they carry an individual grace for the moment. For instance, one might carry a grace for healing from the Father, while another might carry a grace for imparting peace. Each host has a specific grace they are hosting, and the power they release will be unique.

When I was beginning to see in the spirit, a very good friend, who had been seeing in the spirit for years, prayed for me the same prayer Elisha prayed over his assistant's eyes: *"Lord, I pray, open his eyes that he may see"* (2 Kings 6:17). When he prayed, an incredible thing happened to me. I began to see flashes of light all over the room. They were so brilliant that I almost had to close my eyes at one point. My eyes had been opened. I was seeing the brilliance of the heavenly lights in the room that were carrying the grace of the Father. I then saw the way the Father bring His gifts to His children.

> *Every good gift and every perfect gift is from above, and comes down from the **Father of lights**, with whom there is no variation or shadow of turning* (James 1:17).

Hosts appear as lights. They are carrying gifts from the Father. Like a host carrying something contagious, they bring them to the person, who will catch the contagious grace gift they are carrying. There is an interesting moment in the apostle Paul's ministry when he was speaking late into the night and something unusual happens. The Bible reads, *"And there were many lights in the upper chamber, where they were gathered together"* (Acts 20:8 KJV). In passing, this may seem like a normal description of the room, but something so incredibly fascinating is taking place. The hosts in this picture can get lost in translation. Yet, the writer of Acts is not giving a detailed depiction of the interior decorating. Acts is a supernatural book filled with so many miracle moments that we could get lost picking apart every chapter! Perhaps the lights in this story are not simple Christmas lights for a nice Christmas service. Perhaps they are supernatural lights from the Father, hosting God's presence for the pleasure of it!

I remember a moment with a friend at a worship event. We were sitting in the back soaking it all up when I was startled by what my eyes were seeing. The young man on the stage leading worship was so filled with passion, he began waving his arms all around, stirring the crowd with a passion to worship Jesus. As he was waving his arms, I looked up to see what appeared to be rainbow shooting off his arms and shoulders. I did not know that what I was seeing was spiritual and nudged my friend, saying, "Wow, look at that. I don't know how they made rainbows shoot off his shoulders, but the special effects team is on another level here!" My friend looked at me like I was from another planet. He responded, "What rainbows?" I said, "The rainbows on that man's arms! That is amazing!" He shot back, "I am telling you there are no rainbows!" I realized I was seeing the unseen glory of God that was inhabiting the praises of God's people!

FULL COLOR SPECTRUM

One of the things we have noticed about the hosts when they appear is that there is often a color significance to the grace they carry. God is in color. He made color, and He doesn't work in strictly black, white, or manila. He made the sky to appear blue, birds with striking red or yellow feathers, vibrant green fields, and glowing orange sunsets. There are colors around the throne that would blow out of the water the most brilliant colors any high-definition television a company could produce. It's no wonder the enemy wants to impersonate God or even pretend to be an angel of light! The enemy attempts to look like the real thing, much like a fake attempts to imitate an authentically crafted handbag or designer watch. Just because it says Rolex on it doesn't mean it is a Rolex. The difference between a Rolex and a Folex might not be something that a casual observer could see, but the trained eye knows the difference.

And no wonder! For satan himself transforms himself into an angel of light (2 Corinthians 11:14).

What is the difference between the light of a host and the light of an angel? When white light is split by a prism, there are visible colors produced that reveal to us the visible spectrum. We know them as red, orange, yellow, green, blue, indigo, and violet. They make up the seven colors of the rainbow. According to the Book of Revelation, the throne of God is surrounded by a rainbow of color.

SECRETS OF THE SEER

> *Immediately I was in the Spirit; and behold, a throne set in*
> *heaven, and One sat on the throne. And He who sat there*
> *was like a jasper and a sardius stone in appearance; and*
> *there was a rainbow around the throne, in appearance like*
> *an emerald* (Revelation 4:2-3).

The throne of God is brilliantly surrounded with the most gorgeous living color. Seven is a number often used symbolically in Scripture to communicate completion or perfection. God rested on the seventh day from all the work He completed in creating the world (see Gen. 2:2-3). Seven is a number used to describe the Spirit of God as the sevenfold Spirit of God (see Rev. 1:4; 3:1; 4:5; 5:6). Isaiah the prophet lists them for us:

> *The Spirit of the Lord shall rest upon Him, the Spirit of*
> *wisdom and understanding, the Spirit of counsel and might,*
> *the Spirit of knowledge and of the fear of the Lord* (Isaiah
> 11:2).

While God is shining glory with all seven colors of a full spectrum, the enemy is more like dark light. Dark light is light without the full spectrum of visible light. It is ultraviolet, yet not containing the glory of the colors of the spectrum. The enemy does not contain the brilliance of color the Father and His angels have. Therefore, he poses as an angel of light. He cannot display the same brilliance as they do. What's more, the Son of God is the brilliant shining of the Father's glory.

> *God, who at various times and in various ways spoke in*
> *time past to the fathers by the prophets, has in these last days*
> *spoken to us by **His Son**, whom He has appointed heir of all*
> *things, through whom also He made the worlds; who **being***
> ***the brightness of His glory** and the express image of His*

person, and upholding all things by the word of His power, when He had by Himself purged our sins, sat down at the right hand of the Majesty on high (Hebrews 1:1-3).

There is a moment when angels visit that you realize Jesus is close by. There have been times when, in the middle of an angelic visitation, I began to wonder about the glory of Jesus. If the angel is here, where is Jesus? Heavenly beings from God carry a unique holiness on them that makes those who see them immediately desire Jesus. They do not seek to draw glory to themselves but rather seek to glorify the Son. The Son, the Bible says, is more glorious than the angels. As it reads, *"having become so much better than the angels, as He has by inheritance obtained a more excellent name than they"* (Heb. 1:4).

ACTIVATING GOD'S HELPERS

Is there a way we can activate God's helpers? Yes, and often they are waiting on us to do something! What are they waiting for? They are waiting for us to step into the works that expand the Kingdom of God on earth. The psalmist says, *"bless the Lord, you His angels," "bless the Lord, all you His hosts,"* and it follows it all with *"Bless the Lord, all His works, in all places of His dominion"* (Ps. 103:20-22). The Kingdom of God is constantly expanding. The prophet Isaiah saw in his vision a Kingdom that would only increase:

> *Of the increase of His government and peace there will be no end, upon the throne of David and over His kingdom, to order it and establish it with judgment and justice from that time forward, even forever. The zeal of the Lord of hosts will perform this* (Isaiah 9:7).

How does the Kingdom increase? The Kingdom grows in its dominion over everything by the works of God being done on the earth. Angels are on assignment to ensure that God's Kingdom is growing and being assisted and that God is being glorified by the increase of His government and peace. Every time a work of God is done on the earth through one of God's people, the Kingdom of Heaven expands on earth. Each time you or I act of out of generosity, cast a demon off an oppressed soul, speak life over someone, bring healing to a broken heart or body, give to the poor, raise a child in grace and wisdom, or any other work we have been called to do, we help expand the Kingdom of God on earth. When the angels become aware of the works of God being accomplished, they step into a place of action!

UNEMPLOYMENT LINE

I kept seeing angels that were sitting around not doing anything. I did not know what to make of this, and I began to wonder if certain angels were just lazy! It kept happening—when I saw them, they looked bored, like they were in need of something to do! I asked the Holy Spirit, and He spoke to my heart: "These are unemployed angels. They are waiting for a job." I responded, "Are You going to give them one?" He spoke back: "I have given My children stewardship over My works on the earth. When they step out, the angels of God will come out of unemployment and be deployed to assist in the great works I have called each of My children to accomplish." *The people who know their God shall be strong, and carry out great exploits.*" (Dan. 11:32). When God's people step out to expand His Kingdom, we will see angels come to aid of those who are in His service.

ANGELS OF REFRESHING

Every healing comes from the Father, but whom He chooses to use as a conduit is His wisdom. It would be odd to find a king in a kingdom of mankind doing the things he can get his servants to do. Imagine a king who constantly has to jump in and do everything all by himself. Why is it we think God is the only one doing things in His Kingdom? That sounds really odd to me. If God is truly in charge of His Kingdom, I would imagine in His wisdom He is a really phenomenal delegator!

When Jesus, the Son of God, was tested for 40 days in the wilderness, He could have been ministered to by His Father, but something interesting happened. He faced the challenge of the enemy and overcame. The devil threw everything he could at Him at the time but did not overcome Him. At the end of the temptations, He needed refreshing. Who would now minister to Jesus, who had just fought an intense spiritual battle? We read, *"Then the devil left Him, and behold, angels came and ministered to Him"* (Matt. 4:11). Jesus received ministry from the angels! At a later time, Jesus was facing His biggest test yet. He was about to face the test of the cross. In the garden, the battle was raging over the test of His will. Would He do the will of the Father, or would He give in to His humanity and do His own will? He prayed to the Father, *"saying, 'Father, if it is Your will, take this cup away from Me; nevertheless not My will, but Yours, be done.' Then an angel appeared to Him from heaven, strengthening Him"* (Luke 22:42-43). Just as Jesus was strengthened by angels, so can we, as God's children, be. Jesus modeled what was available to us in the New Covenant.

The early monastic fathers wrote about angels in a very positive way.

> ORIGEN (225 A.D.): "Every believer—although the humblest in the Church—is said to be attended by an angel, who the Savior declares always beholds the face of God the Father. Now, this angel has the purpose of being his guardian."[8]

ST. GREGORY THE WONDERWORKER (255 A.D.): "I mean that holy angel of God who fed me from my youth."[9]

ST. ANTONY THE GREAT (300 A.D.): "When you close the doors to your dwelling and are alone you should know that there is present with you the angel whom God has appointed for each man…. This angel, who is sleepless and cannot be deceived, is always present with you; he sees all things and is not hindered by darkness. You should know, too, that with him is God, who is in every place; for there is no place and nothing material in which God is not, since He is greater than all things and holds all men in His hand."[10]

ST. JOHN CLIMACUS (600 A.D.): "In the presence of an invisible spirit, the body becomes afraid; but in the presence of an angel, the soul of the humble is filled with joy. Therefore, when we recognize the presence from the effect, let us quickly hasten to prayer, for our good guardian has come to pray with us."[11]

KEYS TO UNLOCKING THIS SECRET

While we may find ourselves "entertaining angels unaware," we can also be postured to entertain angels knowingly (see Heb. 13:2). This secret is about creating an atmosphere that is inviting to Heaven. The keys to unlocking this secret take us beyond simply being aware that angels exist to living a life filled with angelic activity.

Treat strangers with kindness.

Heaven's messengers may often involve themselves in our life in disguise. The Scriptures tell us, *"Do not neglect to show hospitality to strangers, for by this some have entertained angels without knowing it"* (Heb. 13:2 NASB). The point is not to treat strangers with kindness in the hope that they will reveal themselves as an angel. The point is rather to treat others as you would treat angels because at some point, God will send His angels your way.

Worship God.

Angels love to worship; they live for it. Worshiping the Creator is their primary practice. They are looking for moments to join us in worship. As the psalm reads, *"Praise Him, all His angels; praise Him, all His hosts!"* (Ps. 148:2). When John the revelator fell at the feet of the angel who was showing him around Heaven, the angel opposed his worship and proposed something better: *"And I fell at his feet to worship him. But he said to me, 'See that you do not do that! I am your fellow servant, and of your brethren who have the testimony of Jesus. Worship God! For the testimony of Jesus is the spirit of prophecy'"* (Rev. 19:10). Angels inhabit places of worship to Jesus. When your life is filled with worship, you will attract Heaven's helpers.

Speak God's Word.

Angels perform the Word of God. As the Bible says, *"Bless the Lord, you His angels, who excel in strength, who do His word, heeding the voice of His word"* (Ps. 103:20). Speaking God's Word is about giving it a voice in your life. When angels hear this, they respond. When Daniel sought the Lord for understanding, the angel Gabriel came to deliver a message, saying, *"I have come because of your words"* (Dan. 10:12). Declaring the Word of God brings Heaven to you.

CHAPTER

4

THE SECRET OF IMAGINATION

Now to Him who is able to do exceedingly abundantly above all that we ask or think, according to the power that works in us.

—EPHESIANS 3:20

The true sign of intelligence is not knowledge but imagination.

—ALBERT EINSTEIN

I answered the phone, knowing it was a desperate moment. It was a dear friend calling on behalf of someone in the fourth stage of cancer. The desperation of that moment was tangible. On the other line was a young woman, a mother of children, a faithful wife to a husband, and now a daughter of God who was in desperate need of a miracle. She was calm and full of faith. I spoke into that phone, believing on the other side of the line a miracle was happening. We prayed, asking the Holy Spirit to move and bring healing. The miracle was in the hands of Jesus; all we could do was believe. We declared life over her and spoke to the cancer that it was no longer allowed to remain in the body. It seemed to be a quick and simple payer, but full of faith. We left that phone call trusting God to do a miracle.

It was not long after this that I received a miraculous update. The precious woman for whom we had prayed had been healed from the cancer that was eating away at her body. We were excited to meet face to face at some point in the future!

It was about a year later that we were finally able to sit down over coffee to hear the incredible story of the journey this amazing woman had been on post-healing. As we sat down to listen, I was shocked to discover that an entirely new development in the miracle had emerged! Sitting before my wife and I was an incredible, vibrant, and joy-filled young lady who had discovered the fourth secret—**the secret of imagination**. She proceeded to tell us that a year earlier, the cancer had eaten a hole in the bone of her hip. The missing bone caused complications for her that were serious. Over the course of the year, she would visit her doctor to examine the crater in her hip. One day, she started to use the secret of imagination as a way to connect with God about her need for a miracle. She told me that every day she would sit down and imagine Jesus taking her into her body where

57

the bone had been eaten away. As she stood there with Jesus, she would imagine Him taking putty and placing it into the inner lining where the bone was still there. Over and over she did this, practicing the secret of imagination as a way to connect her hip to the miracle she believed was possible.

About a year went by and she went to her doctor again. The doctor issued a standard X-ray to take a look at the hip and the impact of the cancer. Surprisingly, what came back was one of the most incredible testimonies I have ever heard. Not only did the X-ray reveal the hip bone to be completely whole, but upon further examination, the doctor discovered that new bone had directly grown on top of old bone like a piece from a jigsaw puzzle perfectly designed to fit snug up against the old bone! The doctor was shaken by the entire thing. What was even more incredible was that there appeared to be a hairline division between the old bone and the new bone, and while the old bone looked like it had been around for a while, the new bone appeared to be what the doctor could only describe as "baby bone"! Needless to say, I was stunned by the entire story!

Imagination has become strangely overlooked and grossly undervalued. At the age of five, we have an imagination that is full of life, possibilities, and endless excitement. The world is huge, and anything can become anything in our imagination. My son imagines himself as a Tyrannosaurus Rex most parts of the day, and my daughter imagines herself as a rock star and her cat as the fierce lion that travels with her. These beautiful imaginations are the world of every happy child. By the time we turn 12 we are using less and less of our imagination, and by the time we are adults the progression toward darkness has fully taken over. Our minds, once full of light, life, and abundance, are now filled with limiting knowledge. Knowledge is meant to set the mind free, but the knowledge we learn often has the direct opposite effect. We learn more about what is impossible than about how to think and imagine what is possible. When we bring our minds to God, we begin to be set free from natural thinking, and the imagination begins to soar freely once again. The limits of the imagination begin to be lifted, and we receive in our imagination what could be described as *"ears to hear"* (Mark 4:9). As our imagination begins to be unlocked, we are now open to hear something and see something in our imagination that we might have been closed off to entertaining in times past.

Why is it that we seem to lose our imagination in the deep dark crevices of our soul? The imagination likes to be treated as a priority. When it senses it is not being prioritized, it begins to hide, until we reawaken it and begin to let the light of God shine on us inside the world of the imagination. While our hearts may be beating, our imagination may be sleeping. Like a heart that has stopped beating, some of us may need an energy outside of our natural bodies to wake it up.

THE SPIRIT OF THE MIND

*If indeed you have heard Him and have been taught by Him, as the truth is in Jesus: that you put off, concerning your former conduct, the old man which grows corrupt according to the deceitful lusts, **and be renewed in the spirit of your mind*** (Ephesians 4:21-23).

The mind is a beautiful thing created by God to experience Him in a different way than our bodies or our hearts. In some spiritual environments, the mind has been tossed to the side like a bad relationship. We know it is there, yet we are almost told to leave our minds out of our worship of God so we can experience Him in a greater way. While I am not naïve in knowing the mind can get in the way of God, the seer's secret of imagination is that the mind can

59

be used to experience God in ways beyond the natural world around us. Where does this happen in the mind? Where does the spiritual meet the physical? What is the hidden part of the mind where the imagination intersects with God and man? This is what Paul the apostle referred to as the *"spirit of your mind"* (Eph. 4:23).

Several years ago, the University of Pennsylvania conducted a study on the brain. In the study, they wanted to understand the brain and the neuroscience behind the Pentecostal practice of speaking in tongues. The study, led by Dr. Andrew B. Newberg, was conducted on five praying women who spoke in what the Scriptures call an "unknown language" (see 1 Cor. 14:2). While connected to highly advanced neuroimaging scanners, their brains were studied to see the difference between the images showing the activity of their brains versus those connected to the same scanner who were praying in other religious belief systems. The machine used, single photon emission computed tomography (SPECT), measured blood flow to the brain and therefore brain activity. While those connected to the machine who prayed in strongly held religious beliefs did of course have blood flow to the brain, those who prayed in tongues had a decrease of blood flow to an area of the brain associated with self-control. This indication of activity with a lowered sense of self-control is what caught the attention of the research team. This goes along with what many report as a loss of some level of control and command over the mouth while praying in the Holy Spirit. What was even more amazing to me is that under neuroimaging scans it seemed an area of the brain different to the area typically in charge of communication was the culprit behind the words coming out of the mouth. In an article for *The Atlantic*, Lynne Blumberg writes that *"when practitioners surrender their will, such as when they speak in tongues or function as a medium, activity decreases in their frontal lobes and increases in their thalamus, the tiny brain structure that regulates the flow of incoming sensory information to many parts of the brain. This suggests that their speech is being generated from some place other than the normal speech centers."*[12] What if the area of the brain responsible for spiritual function was the spiritual nature of the mind? I believe it is.

Over centuries of time, we have devolved to using only a small portion of the mind. The seer's secret of imagination is fully awakened when the spirit of the mind is reactivated. What if our mind has hidden abilities to bridge the natural with the supernatural?

THOUGHTS

> *For the weapons of our warfare are not carnal but mighty in God for pulling down strongholds, casting down arguments and every high thing that exalts itself against the knowledge of God,* **bringing every thought into captivity** *to the obedience of Christ* (2 Corinthians 10:4-5).

Thoughts are often overlooked as a subject of spiritual realities. However, the reality is that thoughts often carry a spiritual component to them and have the ability to shape the course of our lives. Every one of us has dealt with the power of negative thoughts. Whether it is a core lie believed or even a positive memory, each of these hidden thoughts has the power to shape the world from our individual perspective. Why have we not allowed the Holy Spirit to help us harness the power of the imagination and teach us the secrets of its potential?

While we may have heard of "taking every thought captive" in regard to controlling negative thoughts, we are also responsible for taking every positive thought captive as well. Thoughts are a primary way God speaks to us, and sometimes we may not know it. That song that might be playing over and over in our head, the new and exciting idea that pops into our brain, or that word that is on our mind upon awakening from a deep sleep—these are all ways that God may be sending a signal our way. And if we learn to take every thought captive, we might even catch the good ones that God is revealing to us as well.

> *For I know the thoughts that I think toward you, says the Lord, thoughts of peace and not of evil, to give you a future and a hope* (Jeremiah 29:11).

Even God has thoughts, and the wild thing about that is He intimately knows the thoughts He has had for each and every living being. Ideas and creativity flood God's imagination, and He is sensitive enough to acknowledge them one by one. The thoughts that He has for each of us anchor us to the wonderful reality that God is planning something really fantastic for each and every one of us. Those thoughts give us hope and peace, something to look forward to. When we become in tune with what God is thinking, we can hear spiritual realities that are based in the mind of God. The secret of imagination helps us unlock these thoughts until His reality becomes ours.

> *But as it is written: "Eye has not seen, nor ear heard, nor have entered into the heart of man things which God has prepared for those who love Him." But God has revealed them to us through His Spirit. For the Sprit searches all things, yes, the deep things of God* (1 Corinthians 2:9-10).

God is preparing things that are so outrageous for us—things that Paul the apostle saw and heard, for he was at one point *"caught up into Paradise and heard inexpressible words, which it is not lawful for a man to utter"* (2 Cor. 12:4). God is preparing things both in this life and in eternity that are so good that Paul later writes, *"Now to him who is able to do immeasurably more than all we ask or imagine, according to his power that is at work within us"* (Eph. 3:20 NIV). Even the furthest reaches of imagination cannot touch the furthest edges of what God is able to do. The secret of imagination unlocks the potential of this promise.

MEDITATION

To deeply understand the secret of imagination we must understand the gift of meditation. While there are numerous books on this subject, and while there are practices of meditation that range from simple mindfulness exercises to the Eastern religious prayerful type, meditation has always been at the center of encountering the supernatural God of Scripture. David writes, *"I will meditate on the glorious splendor of Your majesty, and on Your wondrous works."* (Ps. 145:5).

As the practice of focusing on the revealed knowledge of God in Scripture and the method of rolling over in one's mind the acts of God, meditation takes us into the deep thoughts of God. Mingling our brain power with our spiritual senses, we begin to create a space within the interior life to experience a deeper knowing of God that some would call *yada`*.

יָדַע *yada`*
To know by experience.[13]

Yada` is an ancient Hebrew understanding of knowing that goes beyond knowing someone or something through simple head knowledge. It is a deeper experience that entails knowing in the inner depths of the soul. This type of knowing was experienced in higher practices of meditation that went beyond knowing about God and into experiencing the very essence of His presence. The psalmist writes the following message from God: *"Be still, and know that I am God; I will be exalted among the nations, I will be exalted in the earth!"* (Ps. 46:10).

We can also be comfortable knowing that meditation is not strictly confined to focusing solely on God. We are encouraged to meditate on a wide variety of things that are life giving.

> *Finally, brethren, whatever things are true, whatever things are noble, whatever things are just, whatever things are pure, whatever things are lovely, whatever things are of good report, if there is any virtue and if there is anything praiseworthy—meditate on these things* (Philippians 4:8).

Practice

Some say, "Practice makes perfect." I don't know if "perfect" is exactly what we are getting at, but there is something about practice. Meditation is just that—a practice. It takes consistent daily use to get into a flow state where it will be easy to connect clearly, allowing our imagination to tap into the mind of God. There was a time when I began my journey into meditation that my mind would wander like something had stolen my attention. I would start off using my imagination to connect with God, and suddenly my mind would wander to important yet distracting things. The "monkey mind," as I call it, was taking my brain and going full circus. I would lay down in a very comfortable position such as a hammock or a reclining chair and suddenly be drawn into worrying thoughts over bills or other things—or worse, sleep! We will discuss that quandary in a later chapter, but for now let's stick with what to do when worry arises over legitimate issues.

The tricky thing about the monkey mind is that God actually wants to meet us where we are at. We might walk away from an entire meditation moment and think, "Bad monkey! Bad!" because we became gridlocked into some issue on our mind and couldn't shake it. The beautiful thing we can do in those moments is actually invite God into that space. Why not let Him fill us with thoughts about those things by which we are being moved? If the mind is wandering to bills, or guilt, or even (PG-13 disclaimer) sex, why worry like God is waiting to beat us over the head because we are not thinking straight? We may not be thinking straight, but why not let God participate in those moments to help us get out of "stinking thinking" and into the freedom of encountering Him in the imagination?

At one point, I felt like maintaining a healthy thought life was the last thing that God wanted to help me with. I (hilariously) falsely imagined Him as trying to distance Himself from my thoughts, saying, "You're on your own, buddy!" That just wasn't true. My thoughts are not a performance of my own ability to behave. Yes, I believe in taking every thought captive, but when there is a mountain of self-hatred or something worse on the inside of our thought life, we cannot overcome by simply psyching ourselves up to think better. After all it is *"'not by might nor by power, but by My Spirit,' says the Lord of hosts"* (Zech. 4:6b). The Holy Spirit wants to be just as much a part of the solution and talk to us through the problem. Let Him help you in your weakness, and you can feel confident He will not criticize since He is not a critical spirit. (See James 1:5.)

The other amazing thing that happens in deep meditation with the Lord is that we are not the only one participating. The Holy Spirit is leading us and guiding us through the meditation. When we first start out, it will feel like a chore to get in a peaceful enough place. By the time we are experienced, the ease will have increased and we will begin to enter into holy imaginations, where it is not something we are envisioning on our own—rather, it is something we are yielding to and participating with. The encounter grows from simply mulling over an idea from God to entertaining daydreams with the Lord through internal pictures and visions. It is often in this place that trances occur. Trances are a way that God speaks to us, and it seems that they most often occur in a rested, meditative state.

KEYS TO UNLOCKING THIS SECRET

We can use the secret of imagination in our practice of mediation. Here are some simple steps to help us move forward with this secret:

Use Scripture as a launching pad.

> *blessed is the man who walks not in the counsel of the ungodly, nor stands in the path of sinners, nor sits in the seat of the scornful; but his delight is in the law of the lord, and in his law he meditates day and night. he shall be like a tree planted by the rivers of water, that brings forth its fruit in its season, whose leaf also shall not wither; and whatever he does shall prosper* (Psalm 1:1-3).

When I first began the practice of meditation, I started using Scripture as an incredibly helpful launch pad. It was in these quiet moments that I would ask the Holy Spirit to illuminate my understanding of the Word. Taking a simple Scripture that I had probably heard a dozen times and rolling it over and over in my imagination breathed new life on its value and purpose to me. I might have heard that *"perfect love casts out fear,"* but when I began to meditate on it, a deeper, more personal understanding emerged (see 1 John 4:18).

There was a point in my meditation on the Word where the Holy Spirit began to speak to me some deep meanings behind many of the Scriptures on which I was meditating. It was like in Daniel 5:14, where it is spoken of him: *"I have heard of you, that the Spirit of God is in you, and that light and understanding and excellent wisdom are found in you."* I became aware that during my meditation on the Scriptures, I was being flooded in my innermost being with living light. Understanding was forming in my spirit, and the voice of wisdom would provide me heavenly perspective on the Word of God. The Holy Spirit would walk me line by line through each word. There was a radical point where during this meditation, I would find myself in the Word as if I were immersed in a 4-D living experience of it. It was as if I was there when it was being written and reliving some of the events in the Word on which I was meditating. My imagination was no longer landlocked. I could feel my imagination connecting with God, like He was taking me into the Word on a level I had never experienced before.

Set your mind on things above.

> If then you were raised with Christ, seek those things which are above, where Christ is, sitting at the right hand of God. **Set your mind on things above**, not on things on the earth. For you died, and your life is hidden with Christ in God. When Christ who is our life appears, then you also will appear with Him in glory (Colossians 3:1-4).

The amazing thing about God is He has things and Heaven is filled with them! When I learn to focus on Him, I can also tap into His things. "What things are there?" you might ask. Well, we can look in the window of the Word and find moments where others saw things in Heaven. In the Book of Revelation, John saw living creatures. Ezekiel saw the wheels within a wheel. Isaiah saw the coals of fire on the altar. Each of these pictures shows us something incredible about the nature of God. When I step into the secret of imagination, I set my mind on things above and let God show me new things as well. What else is above? That is for you and me to discover! The good news is, the Father loves to show us all He has.

The other thing that we realize in this secret is the revelation of who we are in Him. I heard of this wild thing that was happening to troops coming back from war. Many of those returning from war with missing limbs and missing body parts were having an experience that medical science described as "phantom pain." While pain really hurts, what they were discovering is that not all pain is actually real. Some of the pain is psychological in nature. Although the injured soldiers had missing limbs, many started reporting that they were having pain in their missing body part. If a soldier had a missing foot, he would report that the foot was giving him terrible pain even though he could see the foot was no longer there. It was as if these soldiers were reliving trauma.

Someone developed a therapeutic cure for these people. It was a breakthrough for the victims of loss. Although nineteenth-century neurologists like Pierre Janet experimented with this treatment, today's developments of this therapy can be traced to Vilayanur S. Ramachandran, a neuroscientist at the University of California, San Diego. The treatment would be known as "mirror therapy." In a standard mirror therapy session, patients perform mirror movements, where the victim watches the reflected image of their intact body part in a mirror. The doctors create an illusory experience with mirrors that gives the victim a view of the missing limb as if it were still there. "Mirror movements," as they are called, are performed by the patient. Though they are aware there limb is missing, the mirror therapy connected to their psyche to the point that many were reporting massively reduced pain.

The principle of seeing one's self in a healed way applies to us even in meditation. We are told, *"seek those things which are above, where Christ is...your life is hidden with Christ in God. When Christ who is our life appears, then you also will appear with Him in glory"* (Col. 3:1, 3-4). As we meditate on Christ, something wonderful happens. He begins to show us our true self in Him! Our imagination is lit up with a healthy and whole vision of who we are in Christ. What does this do to our failed understanding of who we are? I propose to you that many of us are carrying around phantom pain rooted in lies we believe about ourselves. Some of the lies include, "I am worthless. I am a terrible person. I am a liar, an addict, a _____." You fill in the blank. Each of those lies are overcome as we see who He is and envision who we are in Him!

CHAPTER
5

THE SECRET OF
THE SENSES

But solid food belongs to those who are of full age, that is, those who by reason of use have their senses exercised to discern both good and evil.

—HEBREWS 5:14

Don't ignore the five senses in search of a sixth.

—BRUCE LEE

I was lying on my back having a nice afternoon nap when I heard my friend shouting with frustration. I was kind of in between sleep and consciousness. His shouting outside continued to grow. In the middle of this, I felt a tiny sensation from the presence of God on my left arm. I knew this was a breakthrough moment. For years, I was forming a relational language with God that was beyond words. It felt like sign language between us. I had encountered this feeling before. It was God saying He wanted to give a breakthrough for the moment. I got up to go outside and found my friend in a panic. "What's up?" I asked gently. "My tire is busted, and I have to replace it," he responded. I assured him that I was there for him. "So let's replace it. I will help you. Do you have a spare in the trunk?" Exhausted and overwhelmed, he shot back, "Yes, but the wheel nut won't budge. I have been at this for an hour trying to get this off! Nothing is working. I have to be at work or I am going to lose my job!" He got up and stood on the tire iron with his full body weight, and the thing still wouldn't budge. I was amazed. I knew I couldn't do any more than my friend was doing with his own strength. He needed a breakthrough. The wheel nut was completely locked on the wheel, and we could not get it off.

Have you ever worked so hard on a peanut butter sandwich and then you just could not open the jar of jelly? Your wife walks over all nonchalant and says, "Let me try!" and opens it on her first attempt! "I have been upstaged," you think. This was not one of those moments. I told my friend, "God is going to give you a breakthrough. Let's pray." He responded with a lack of faith, "What is that going to do! This thing is locked!" We prayed one time, "Thank You, Father, for breakthrough! We come together for breakthrough! Let this wheel nut move!" He picked up the tire iron again and put it to the wheel nut again. He secured the tire iron on it, mumbling under his breath how this was not going to work. As he shifted the tire iron, he could not believe what was happening. A miracle had moved that wheel. It was a breakthrough moment that all started with a gentle nudge from the Father on my elbow.

"Why the elbow?" you might ask. As simple as it sounds, seers have a language developed over time between the Holy Spirit and them. The language is not simple English, Spanish, Italian, or even Hebrew. The language is the other things that are not spoken with words but are spoken with what you and I would call body language. Understanding that God speaks to each one of us in deeper ways than words, we find ourselves in another secret from the seer—**the secret of the senses**.

Every one of us has different senses that are more heightened in acuity than the others. One might have a much stronger sense of smell than they do sight, while another might have a stronger sense of taste than feeling. Everyone is unique, yet all of us have senses that are designed by the Creator to experience the invisible world. When the Father created humanity, He did it with the intention that every single one of our senses would be able to interact in the natural as well as the supernatural world. We are designed to experience God with all five senses: taste, touch, smell, sight, and hearing. The misunderstanding is thinking that every seer operates only by the visionary way of sight. Seers see, yet they see not only with eyes; they see with all the other senses as well. It may sound strange, but seers can perceive with their sense of smell, their sense of touch, their sense of hearing, and their sense of taste.

Taste is one of the most wonderful senses created by God. Every day, billions of people across the planet are revived to life by their favorite hot morning beverage. Whether tea, coffee, or something else, that sensation of taste alerts the body that there is an incredible day ahead. It gives the body a knowing, a sense that wakes the soul for whatever is to come its way. Often the seer is not seeing with the eyes but seeing with taste and the other senses. This is the secret of the senses! We are designed by the Creator to use our sense of taste, touch, hearing, etc., to *see* the world around us. Let's go into the depths of what each of these senses looks like and discover living examples of this secret in action.

TASTE

Oh, taste and see that the Lord is good; blessed is the man who trusts in Him! (Psalm 34:8)

The average person has about 10,000 taste buds, and amazingly they are replaced just about every two weeks. Taste accounts for the most pleasurable experiences as a human being. When a child experiences a new taste for the first time—the first sugary treat or the first salty snack—it's eye opening! As we grow up, our palate matures and we desire certain tastes. The late night craving for something delicious might be driving us to explore areas of the refrigerator we would not typically dare go. We say to ourselves, "I know there is chocolate here somewhere!" What a great way for the Holy Spirit to get our attention. Taste is a wonderful gift with which we can experience God!

There was a fascinating moment where God was moving on my heart to fast and pray. I don't enjoy fasting; in fact, I can't stand it! I have friends who love the discipline of fasting, but I am not one of them. So, I did the fast with a purpose of laying aside natural comforts to experience a different side of Jesus. This was a longer fast, and I decided to refrain from everything except water. During the first week, I was over at a friend's house and we decided to worship. While deep into worship, I felt the Holy Spirit move upon me in an unusual way. I was brought into a deep place of connection, experiencing the love of God. At that moment, I started to taste honey on my lips. It was the distinct flavor of honey, and I knew I had not been drinking anything except water! I sat there in the presence of God, licking my lips, completely amazed. While the presence of God surrounded me in that moment, I asked the Holy Spirit to help me understand what was happening. I felt impressed by the Holy Spirit that I would find what I was looking for in the Scriptures. I searched, and I found it:

> *Your lips, O my spouse, drip as the honeycomb; honey and milk are under your tongue; and the fragrance of your garments is like the fragrance of Lebanon* (Song of Solomon 4:11).

Taste gives us an ability to see from a different lens. There are times it is sweet, and there are times when God uses our sense of taste to experience something bitter or disgusting in order to get our attention for other reasons. For instance, if I taste something bitter in my mouth, I begin to wonder if I am sensing and seeing a root of bitterness in a situation I am in. God can use taste many different ways, and I am always learning and experiencing something new— and that keeps me searching for answers.

SIGHT

> *I will stand my watch and set myself on the rampart, and watch to see what He will say to me, and what I will answer when I am corrected* (Habakkuk 2:1).

Sight is another way the secret of the senses operates in a seer. As much sense as that makes, we can miss the other side of sight. The wild thing about sight is that God has given to each one of us two sets of eyes. No, I don't mean two eyeballs. I mean two sets of eyes. Our first set of eyes is the two visible eyes that you and I have to see the world around us. If we are blessed with good vision, we see without trouble the beauty and the wonder of all creation. Yet there are other ways to see, and that takes a different set of eyes.

When we look at the picture of the throne of God in Revelation 4, before the throne of God there are quite a number of unusual happenings. The throne is surrounded with 24 other thrones and 24 elders on those thrones casting their crowns down day and night (see Rev. 4:4). The seven Spirits of God are burning before the throne like lamps of fire (see Rev. 4:5). One of the stranger things happening at the throne are the living creatures. There are four living creatures, and each has a different face. *"The first living creature was like a lion, the second living creature like a calf, the third living creature had a face like a man, and the fourth living creature was like a flying eagle"* (Rev. 4:7). While each of these creatures carry their own meaning, something is very interesting about all four. Each of them have eyes literally in the back of their head, but what is also interesting is they also have another set of eyes (see Rev. 4:6).

> *The four living creatures, each having six wings, **were full of eyes around and within**. And they do not rest day or night, saying: "Holy, holy, holy, Lord God Almighty, who was and is and is to come!"* (Revelation 4:8)

The living creatures have eyes on the outside, both in front and in back, and they have another set of eyes—the eyes within. The eyes within are the eyes of the heart. They are the invisible eyes created by God to see invisible things. In order to look at the invisible world, we must have a different set of eyes. These are known as "the eyes of our heart." Paul, the writer of a majority of the New Testament, was aware of these eyes and prayed for an incredible grace to give to the Church that would cause the eyes of their heart to see.

For this reason I too, having heard of the faith in the Lord Jesus which exists among you and your love for all the saints, do not cease giving thanks for you, while making mention of you in my prayers; that the God of our Lord Jesus Christ, the Father of glory, may give to you a spirit of wisdom and of revelation in the knowledge of Him. I pray that the eyes of your heart may be enlightened, so that you will know what is the hope of His calling, what are the riches of the glory of His inheritance in the saints, and what is the surpassing greatness of His power toward us who believe. These are in accordance with the working of the strength of His might which He brought about in Christ, when He raised Him from the dead and seated Him at His right hand in the heavenly places, far above all rule and authority and power and dominion, and every name that is named, not only in this age but also in the one to come (Ephesians 1:15-21 NASB).*

The eyes of the heart being enlightened can sound very symbolic, but it is the original language that reveals something deeper and more important to us that is taking place in this prayer. In the original Greek text, the word *eyes* and the word *heart* are translated literally. The words do not need much explanation, as they are translated into modern language as it already is; *eyes* mean "eyes" and *heart* means "heart." However, it is the word *enlightened* used here that is a game changer when we recognize its meaning to us. The Greek word used here for *enlightened* is *phōtizō*. Often this word is used in other places as "light" or "illuminated." *Phōtizō* is also the basis of the word *photo*. When the Spirit of Wisdom and Revelation are manifest in someone and they are enlightened, what happens is much like a photo flash. They have a spark of God's light, and when that hits the spirit, the result is a picture imprinted on the imagination. The picture is a glimpse into the unseen—sometimes parabolic, other times literal. It is a small glimpse into three areas of God's infinite knowing. What are those areas? Well, the Scripture expands upon this and tells us three areas for which we are given sight and insight.

1. *"The hope of His calling"* (Ephesians 1:18).

The hope of His calling is the fullness of the call the Father, Son, and Spirit have, both for themselves and for all of created order. When the Spirit of Wisdom and Revelation are imparted, we begin to see the great story of God that is being told and the ever-increasing revelation of His goodness toward mankind. Ask the Father to let you see into the hope of His calling and give you flash photo images that let you see how great the calling is.

2. *"The riches of the glory of His inheritance in the saints"* (Ephesians 1:18).

God has riches that are His to give out. The beautiful thing is that God is generous, and He loves to give to His kids. When we are filled with the Spirit of Wisdom and Revelation, with sight and insight, we are given glimpses into the things that God is giving to every one of us. The inheritance is the wonderful gifts Jesus is giving to each of us. Therefore, He says: *"When He ascended on high, He led captivity captive, and gave gifts to men"* (Eph. 4:8). The gifts of His Spirit are the riches of the glory of His inheritance. Ask Jesus to give you eyes to see the gifts and the inheritance He has given you through His resurrection and ascension.

3. *"The surpassing greatness of His power toward us who believe"* (Ephesians 1:19).

God is powerful, and His power is toward us, not against us. He wants to empower us and give us that Samson-like strength to live a victorious life. The power of God is the Holy Spirit. Jesus calls Him *"the finger of God,"* and God has more power in His finger than all the powers of the enemy (see Luke 11:20). The power of God comes upon us to help us live the victorious life in Christ. Ask Holy Spirit to give you a picture image of the power of God coming upon your life. This image will be a vision of the strength of His presence that He is pouring out on us as we believe.

SMELL

> *Now thanks be to God who always leads us in triumph in Christ, and through us diffuses the **fragrance** of His knowledge in every place* (2 Corinthians 2:14).

The fragrance of God manifests as we follow Christ's lead into victory. Several years back, I was struggling with intense allergies. I was doing a ton of research on what might be causing my allergic reactions. I could not find breakthrough and was on over-the-counter medicine that was wrecking my system. As the allergies continued to worsen, so did I. I found myself looking forward to sleep, as it might be the only way of escaping from the allergies of the day. I had prayed often and received prayer for healing. I was fighting for a breakthrough.

While enjoying dinner with some company one night, they asked if I would be willing to pray for their kids coming back from school. I was happy to do so and felt in my spirit these high schoolers were about to have a very powerful encounter with the Holy Spirit. When they got to the house, the dad stepped out and told the kids that I was willing to pray for them. We went into the family room and began to minister with prophetic power. My wife reached out her hand to pray for a young lady for whom she felt God had given her a prophetic word. I watched, supportively praying for breakthrough for this young lady, while a couple of the young guys were waiting to be prayed for next. While praying and waiting, I could see out of the corner of my eye an angel from God appear in the corner of the room. It shocked me, and in that instant I had a deep knowing that a very special miracle was about to happen in that room!

As my wife finished praying, I felt faith to ask God for the greater miracle. It was as if I was tangibly aware of a faith to move mountains. I spoke up and said, "God is about to do a special miracle!" I asked if anyone at the home could find for me unscented olive oil. I made sure to repeat twice that I needed *unscented* olive oil for the miracle I had faith that God was going to do. Before I stepped out in faith, I asked everyone to smell the oil in the bottle to make sure that the oil was verifiably unscented. Everyone who smelled it agreed it was unscented olive oil. When I reached out to pray, I poured a little out on one of the young guy's hands in front of me. I prayed, "God, I ask that You would change this into Your favorite fragrance. In Jesus' name!" In that moment, the unscented olive oil was transformed into the fragrance of a rosebush mixed with laundry detergent! It was so potent; the fragrance began to fill the air. While I stood there stunned and in awe, others around me started dropping to their knees, crying at the glory of that moment. The fragrance of Heaven had invaded that place. I did not know what to do, so I did the only thing that came to my mind: "smell it." I put my hand in the oil and pulled it to my nose. When I did, I could feel the fragrance moving through the breathing passages of my nose up into the sinus cavities in my face. A hot, burning sensation was going through my face, and I could smell the rich sweetness of that fragrance as I breathed it in. It was in that moment that I was healed of allergies. The sinus allergies that I had been afflicted with for the last five years immediately stopped and have not returned ever since!

Think about it for a second. The high priest goes into the temple every year for the people. Once a year, one priest is chosen to represent all the tribes and go before the manifest glory of God at the meeting space of the Holy of Holies. As he enters into the Holy of Holies, above the gold-covered mercy seat and in between the two covering cherubim is the cloud of God's glory, the manifest presence of the person of God. Now, the temple was already filled with the fragrant aroma from the altar of incense, but just past the altar of incense, beyond the veil, hung the glory of God Himself! Imagine the beauty, the majesty! Imagine the smells! I can imagine the fragrance of God being better than anything we could ever imagine!

With the secret of the senses, the seer sees with the nose just as powerfully as the eyes. Certain smells give us a sense of what God is up to. Some smells are good and life giving. They touch us in a deep way, like aromatherapy. Other smells are disgusting and remind us of something gross. There are times in worship when I smell the beautiful fragrance of Jesus and I know He is near. I may not be able to see Him with my eyes, but I have sensed Him with a different seer activation. At other times, I will sense a demonic presence, and it smells foul. It may remind me of sulfur or mildew. These are signs to us that this secret is revealing that the source of the problem is not a practical problem; it is demonic. When I sense that foul smell, I cannot counsel the problem out of something or someone; it has to be dealt with through prayer.

TOUCH

But as He went, the multitudes thronged Him. Now a woman, having a flow of blood for twelve years, who had spent all her livelihood on physicians and could not be healed by any, came from behind and touched the border of His garment. And immediately her flow of blood stopped. And Jesus said, "Who touched Me?" When all denied it, Peter and those with him said, "Master, the multitudes throng and

press You, and You say, 'Who touched Me?'" But Jesus said,
"Somebody touched Me, for I perceived power going out from
Me" (Luke 8:42-46).

In the secret of the senses, touch is an incredible way for us to see the unseen. Jesus was touched, but it was not like every other touch. Everyone around him was pushing in on Him, touching Him, but He could discern one specific touch. The moment this desperate lady touched Him in faith, she was healed. Her touch was not just another natural touch. She had touched a place in the Spirit that was able to draw power out of Jesus and bring healing to her body. If the sense of touch is a place we can encounter the Kingdom of God, what is He trying to convey to us?

Now, this is a unique use of the senses, because some of what you are about to read is highly subjective. I do not think that everything is objective in the Kingdom, meaning I believe much of the prophetic language we encounter from God is very specific to the individual and his or her interpretation of that language. For instance, Jesus spit in a blind man's eye and made him whole, yet He did not spit again (see Mark 8:23). Why would He do this? In that day, spitting on someone was a form of mockery. The blind were often mocked by others in those days, and every time they were spit on it was like someone was saying, "You are cursed." Jesus spits on this person and touches him. He cannot see, but he can feel; and the very thing that was usually done as a curse to this man, Jesus used to heal him.

As I learned this secret, the Holy Spirit began revealing to me different ways of seeing with touch that are now a language that He uses with me to help know what He is doing. Often when I pray with someone for healing, either I or the person being ministered to will experience heat. This rise in temperature is not just a sudden hot flash of the body. It is a sign that His presence is near and He is bringing healing. Habakkuk 3:5 tells us that *"fever followed at His feet."* At other times, it will feel like electricity is moving through my hands while praying for someone or something. With this type of touch experience, I have seen miracles happen. I began to ask the Holy Spirit some time ago about this, and He spoke to me in a dream. In the dream, I was shown that when heat is appearing, it is a sign of healing presence being released. In the same dream I was given, I was also shown that when electric-like power shows up while praying, whether I can feel it on my hands or my head, it is a sign of breakthrough miracles. These little touch clues give me an understanding of what the Father wants and how the Holy Spirit is ministering when it happens.

HEARING

*The **hearing ear** and the seeing eye, the Lord has made them both* (Proverb 20:12).

It may sound strange, but one of the most premier seer prophets in the Scripture had to learn how to hear God's voice using only his ears. This revelation to Elijah was the most profound of all the encounters of which he was a part.

Then He said, "Go out, and stand on the mountain before the Lord." And behold, the Lord passed by, and a great and strong wind tore into the mountains and broke the rocks in pieces before the Lord, but the Lord was not in the wind; and after the wind an earthquake, but the Lord was not in the earthquake; and after the earthquake a fire, but the Lord was not in the fire; and after the fire a still small voice. So it was, when Elijah heard it, that he wrapped his face in his mantle and went out and stood in the entrance of the cave. Suddenly a voice came to him, and said, "What are you doing here, Elijah?" (1 Kings 19:11-13)

We have been given ears, but that does not necessarily mean that we are using them. Jesus would say it like this: *"But blessed are your eyes for they see, and your ears for they hear"* (Matt. 13:16). Having hearing ears is important, and so we must pay attention to the things being heard. Some things we hear are more pronounced, yet others are more like the whispering voice that spoke to Elijah. As we grow in our ability to hear, we will be able to discern even the slightest thing that God is trying to speak to us. There are multiple ways that hearing happens. Sometimes we hear internally, and this type of hearing is subtler than other ways. At other times we hear outwardly, and this is clearer and much more in our face. Either way, we can recognize hearing is a vital means for us to receive what God is speaking to us.

With the secret of the senses, hearing happens not only with God's voice speaking directly through us. Hearing also happens as we pay attention to the world around us and the thoughts inside us. There are times when hearing a song on the radio may be more than coincidence. Music and lyrics can be a primary way that hearing happens within this secret. I have walked into a place knowing that God wanted to provide a breakthrough and suddenly I will hear the radio in that place playing a song with lyrics that are exactly what I needed to hear in that moment. At other times, I will be going about my day and suddenly a song will be stuck in my head that I never sing. This song will be the exact revelation of what is going on in the moment we are in. It will be like this song is shedding light and uncovering what is going on beneath the surface. Pay attention to the songs that you happen to be singing in your heart—they may be the Holy Spirit speaking to you with the secret of the senses!

KEYS TO UNLOCKING THIS SECRET

The secret of the senses is a beautiful mystery that reveals how human nature can connect with divine nature. One of these areas of the senses may be stronger than the other in your life, but it may be an opportunity to explore and grow in each of these areas.

Practice the senses.

> *But solid food belongs to those who are of full age, that is, those who by reason of use have their senses exercised to discern both good and evil* (Hebrews 5:14).

When we practice using our senses to see into the supernatural, we will begin to grow in this area. It is in having our "senses exercised" that we become more aware of when it is happening. Take some time in each day to dial in to one area of the senses to see what it is conveying to you. If it is touch, turn off your focus on the other areas and become aware of the different things you are picking up with touch. Often when I am doing this, I may feel a heat touching my left ear or a subtle sense of God's presence focused in on my hand. As these things become more common, you will begin to understand what God is trying to convey.

Raise self-awareness.

> *Then Moses said, "I will now turn aside and see this great sight, why the bush does not burn"* (Exodus 3:3).

Pay attention to the small things. I am not suggesting your whole day gets shifted by one little moment, but even Moses had to stop and see the burning bush. Become self-aware about what the Holy Spirit is doing in you. As you do, you will become more in touch with the unique ways God is speaking to you.

Keep a journal.

> *And Joshua put these words on **record**, writing them in the book of the law of God; and he took a great stone, and put it up there under the oak-tree which was in the holy place of the Lord* (Joshua 24:26 BBE).

When we keep a record, we are honoring what has happened to us. It is a way of creating history with God. As we encounter God in the secret of the senses, some of the experiences we will have will be difficult to understand at first. Recording these moments will give us the ability to study the before and after. What is the fruit or the result of this encounter? This is a great question that we can ask ourselves as we value these seer secrets and write them down.

CHAPTER
6

THE SECRET
OF HUMANITY

And without controversy great is the mystery of godliness: God was manifested in the flesh, justified in the Spirit, seen by angels, preached among the gentiles, believed on in the world, received up in glory.

—1 TIMOTHY 3:16

Being human is given, but keeping our "humanity" is a choice.

—UNKNOWN

A toxic lie was once spreading through the Church. It was a battle the first-century Church had to face head on because it questioned one of the most important components of our faith. The greatest heresy in the early Church was not the issue of tongues or the issue of whether a Spirit-filled believer could possibly have a demon oppressing or even possessing them. This would question the very foundation of our faith: *Did Jesus come in the flesh?*

At some point, the issue arose because a certain teaching had swept through the community of God's people. The teaching that was at the core of this heresy was that all flesh is evil. If all flesh being evil was the core lie, imagine the ripple effect within the Church. If that is true, how could Christ have possibly come in the flesh? As the teaching spread, the question became: Did Christ really rise from the dead, and if so, did it happen in His body or is His body still in the grave and He is now Spirit? This message questioned everything about the fundamentals of our faith. Paul, the main contributor to the New Testament, challenges this new teaching (see 1 Cor. 15:14).

As the doctrine was challenged, the deception that swept through the Church created bad fruit that went way beyond the core issue. Fast-forward two thousand years and we have a set of beliefs that question our spirituality when we are faced with our humanity. How many spiritual people have I been around who simply do not know how to be human! This brings us to the sixth secret—**the secret of humanity**.

No doubt, being human is a challenging thing. Perhaps you have heard yourself say at one point, "I am only human." This usually follows a moment of stupidity on our part, but we are doing our best to move forward. While this may sound true, the reality of who we are in Christ is something so much more. Being human does not mean we have fallen from grace into this strange condition called humanity.

God masterfully created us in His image and His likeness. The secret of humanity is perhaps one of the most powerful secrets of the seer because it deals with the core issue of who we are.

We are human, and this may sound like a difficult truth, but the wonder of it all is that God didn't screw up the first time in His creation. We are His original design, and He considered it such a good one that He sent His Son and brought Him forth into this world not as an angel, but as a human being with eyes, ears, heart, lungs, soul—just like us. Humans were the original design, hardwired to interact with God just as we are.

You see, Jesus did not come to do away with humanity to create a new race; He came to restore us to being fully human again with a fully alive spirit, a healthy soul, and a body filled with the resurrection life of Jesus. Adam and Eve were originally designed to live fully alive, but when they ate from the tree of the knowledge of good and evil something happened to their being: death came in. However, when Jesus came to give His own life for ours, death was dealt with on the cross. He took the punishment of sin and death in His body so we could be given life more abundantly in ours. So, what does it look to be human? Let's explore this wonderful secret—the secret of humanity.

LOST AND FOUND

And they heard the sound of the Lord God walking in the garden in the cool of the day, and Adam and his wife hid themselves from the presence of the Lord God among the trees of the garden. Then the Lord God called to Adam and said to him, "Where are you?" (Genesis 3:8-9)

Adam and Eve lost something in the Fall. Before this tragic moment, mankind enjoyed uninterrupted access to the Godhead.

Their unique place within the created order gave them authority over all creation, and this authority came from their connection to the Father. God walked with Adam and Eve, lovingly guiding them through this brand-new world. But something happened in the Fall that would change everything. Before the Godhead made it to the point of talking to Adam and Eve about their sin, a question is formed. Something that had not yet been spoken was now being asked: *"Where are you?"* (Gen. 3:9).

To truly understand, we have to ask ourselves, "What is making God ask this question in this way?" Someone once said, "If God asks a question, it is not because He does not know the answer." Mankind was made in the image of God and with the likeness of God and was given access to heavenly places. This unique access made humans extremely different than the rest of creation. Adam and Eve not only were made to dwell on earth with creation, but they were created to live in Heaven with the Father at the same time. We sometimes have misunderstood Heaven as something created for us to go to when we die as though it was created as a result of the Fall. The record in Genesis tells us that Heaven was created before the Fall, on the first day of creation. If this is true and Heaven was not initially created for eternal life insurance, what was its original purpose?

I have a phone. It's an amazing and powerful little pocket computer with massive amounts of memory. I used to think its storage capabilities were almost limitless until I took way too many pictures, causing me now to get regular notices that my phone is full. What happens when you have all these incredible photos of the wife and kids, the dog, the cat, and you do not want to delete any of them, even though most of them are multiple copies of the same photo? You put them in the cloud. For the tech-challenged folks reading this, "the cloud" is a term used to describe a digital hosting platform that will take all the photos off the cell phone and upload them into an online storage facility—the cloud.

I want to propose to you that Heaven was originally made as a place to hold all the resources and things for which earth would not have enough space. This would be the environment in which God would keep every spiritual blessing that would one day be completely unlocked for those in Christ. *"Blessed be the God and Father of our Lord Jesus Christ, who has blessed us with every spiritual blessing in the heavenly places in Christ"* (Eph. 1:3). Now, in Christ we have been restored to what was once lost in the fall of man. You see, Adam and Eve were originally created to be seated in heavenly places with God, while at the same time growing the family of mankind on earth. So when God asked Adam where he was, it was not because He did not know where Adam was on earth; it was because He could no longer see Adam in heavenly places. Fast-forward many thousands of years, and Christ would restore man's place back to the seat Adam and Eve once occupied. When Jesus came, it was God's message to us, saying, "I have come to get My kids back!"

> *But God, who is rich in mercy, because of His great love with which He loved us, even when we were dead in trespasses, made us alive together with Christ (by grace you have been saved), and raised us up together, and made us sit together in the heavenly places in Christ Jesus* (Ephesians 2:4-6).

What was lost has now been found. Jesus has restored access to Heaven with humanity itself. By dying on the cross, He used His own humanity to pay for our sins and bring us back into right relationship with the Father. This incredible act of love has unlocked something for you and me that begins at salvation but does not stop there. Not only are we given an opportunity for forgiveness; we are also raised, resurrected, and seated at the right hand of God in Christ in heavenly places.

The secret of humanity reveals to us that being human is not designed to keep us from God, but to bring us closer to Him. It gives us access to heavenly places. While we may have two feet here on the earth, we can also have our head in the cloud. Humanity is the only creation designed to be able to handle this tension. Angels move in and out of the spiritual world and the physical world, but we were created in God's image with a higher capacity to operate in both worlds simultaneously.

The secret of humanity embraces the fact that while our head may be in the cloud, we can also be grounded and embrace the physical and emotional qualities of our humanity at the same time. Seers who understand this will operate at a higher level of seeing because they will see not only in the spirit, but also in the natural. What is it we can understand that will help us embrace this wonderful humanity? Let's open up this mystery and take a look at what makes us human.

SPIRIT-SOUL-BODY

Then God said, "Let Us make man in Our image, according to Our likeness; let them have dominion over the fish of the sea, over the birds of the air, and over the cattle, over all the earth and over every creeping thing that creeps on the earth" (Genesis 1:26).

When God created us, He did so knowing that He was going to give us something He would give to nothing else in His creation; He was going to give us His likeness and His image. God, speaking with Himself, developed a plan. This plan would entail handing the keys of leadership over this new earth to man. Man was called to steward this new creation and fully develop what God had put into place. For this great task, man would need to be a unique creation, something unlike any other piece of God's handiwork. He needed to be like God in some way. For man to carry the most God-like qualities, he would be created with three main components: spirit, soul, and body.

The combination of these three things makes us incredibly unique and gives us something no other part of creation has. We experience life from three different places. We experience life first from our spirit. At the core of who we are, we are spiritual beings. Our spirit knows there is more to life, and so we look for experiences beyond the physical world around us because our spirit longs for those realities. Jesus spoke to the woman at the well about this reality. In His journey, we find Jesus sitting at a well with a Samaritan woman who came to retrieve water. She pushed back only because her kind, the Samaritans, did not interact with His kind, the Jews. When she pushes back, Jesus responds with an invitation.

> *A woman of Samaria came to draw water. Jesus said to her, "Give Me a drink." For His disciples had gone away into the city to buy food. Then the woman of Samaria said to Him, "How is it that You, being a Jew, ask a drink from me, a Samaritan woman?" For Jews have no dealings with Samaritans. Jesus answered and said to her, "If you knew the gift of God, and who it is who says to you, 'Give Me a drink,' you would have asked Him, and He would have given you living water"* (John 4:7-10).

The spirit is thirsty for something that cannot be satisfied with any earthy element. People run for years, searching for a way to satisfy the deep thirst within the spirit, trying to fill it with material things and thinking they will fulfill that invisible longing in their hearts. The problem we soon run into is realizing we cannot fill invisible things with physical answers. We will quickly find ourselves thirsting again.

> *Jesus answered and said to her, "Whoever drinks of this water will thirst again, but whoever drinks of the water that I shall give him will never thirst. But the water that I shall give him will become in him a fountain of water springing up into everlasting life" (John 4:13-14).*

The spirit is thirsting for something that cannot be met by anything in this world. How do we get that thirst met? Like the woman at the well, we ask, *"Sir, give me this water, that I may not thirs..."* (John 4:15).

SOUL

In the secret of humanity, every seer needs to realize the other part of our nature. God created us in His image—not just with a spirit, but also with a soul. The difference between these two is that while our spirit contains our spiritual capacity, the soul contains our emotional capacity. When we have a healthy soul and spirit working together, we come into a place of harmony in our life where our spirit, soul, and body can experience the goodness of God in life around us.

> *Beloved, I pray that you may prosper in all things and be in health, just as your soul prospers (3 John 1:2).*

The secret of humanity understands the soul's vital place in life. Unfortunately, even our spirituality has done a terrible work at neglecting the soul. We might say, "Praise the Lord" all day, but deep inside we are a wreck because we have overlooked the soul's deep needs and replaced it with hyperspirituality. My red flags go up when

I am around someone who says something spiritual every other sentence but they are aging quicker than the day. How did we get so spiritual but our life can still be an absolute mess?

I have spent many nights in my adult life in prayer lines praying for people with real needs. There was a time in my ministry where night after night, meeting after meeting, I would be praying for people, telling them what God is showing me about their life or praying for healing. During those times, there were moments when I was aware that the anointing was high, I was seeing accurately and prophesying accurately, but like a fuel gauge in my car I could tell my soul was on "E." I was getting short with folks and began rushing, not being patient enough or present enough. In the middle of praying, my mind would start wandering off to other things and other places. What was happening? My soul needed some TLC—tender loving care.

Just as we try make the mistake of answering our spiritual longing with material things, we can also make the mistake of answering the soul's needs with things that never seem to refresh us. When anxiety hijacks the emotions and panic becomes a crisis we have to manage on a daily basis, something is off and we have neglected to care for the state of our soul. We might daydream all day of escaping on some grand vacation where we can finally unwind, or find ourselves obsessively looking at our retirement. These moments are indicators that our soul is saying, "Please help!" The soul is crying for attention and desiring a place of connectivity so that it can recharge and refresh. The question we have to ask is, how do we recharge and refresh our soul when we feel like we have given so much of ourselves to so many things around us? Do we have a way of recharging that makes our emotional capacity come alive again?

INTO-ME-YOU-SEE

The secret of humanity reveals something in each of us—the deep desire for an intimate connection with the person of God. We may not see it if we look in the mirror, but there is a God-shaped hole in our soul. Filling this hole is the primary motivator in our life. Sex, drugs, music, food—we gorge our self on things that give us a moment of escape from facing that missing invisible reality. After a binge or two or three, we find our soul at a dead end and are forced to realize there is no way out unless we come face to face with the need we have in this inner person. What we are truly looking for, more than anything else, is intimacy. We may trick ourselves into thinking that what we really need is that hot new car with that new car smell, a little fling with the girl in the office, money, power—you get the idea. Yet at the end of all these things, no matter how thrilling they are, we end up with a need that can only be met by a deeper connection.

Because we were made in the image of God, our humanity longs for a connection to divinity. We crave intimacy with the Creator because He is the one whole truly knows us in the core of our inner person. He knows us in a way even our mothers who carried us over a period of nine months do not even know. He speaks, *"Before I formed you in the womb I knew you; before you were born I sanctified you"* (Jer. 1:5). This deep knowing is what we have imprinted on our souls before we are even born, and it is what we keep searching for until we find it. I like to look at intimacy as "into-me-you-see." The place of intimate connection is found when we feel like someone is seeing us in a way that connects to who we are on our deepest level. To be seen is not to be looked at. We look at people every day, and people look at us. But do they see who we really are? And do we experience an unconditional love that our heart and soul craves? We are often like a battery that is drained from the issues of life: screaming kids, stressful work environments, the pressures of life. Yet Jesus' voice still speaks to us today: *"Come to Me, all you who labor and are heavy laden, and I will give you rest. Take My yoke upon you and learn from Me, for I am gentle and lowly in heart, and you will find rest for your souls. For My yoke is easy and My burden is light"* (Matt. 11:28-30). He longs to fulfill the desire of being known with a care and love that nothing else will satisfy. We find this intimacy, or into-me-you-see, being met when we rest in Him.

What would it look like if the central focus of our pursuit of encounters was to see Jesus? Personally, I am far more interested in seeing Jesus than an angel or something else in Heaven. My prayer over and over was, *"I want to see Jesus. Let me see Jesus. Show me Your face, Jesus."* When I did see Him, the first thing I noticed was His eyes. I remember they could see into me and I was not afraid. Those eyes saw everything—my sin, my issues, my failures—and yet they saw that those things were not me. Those eyes saw the real me, and it changed me. This is what being a seer is all about—looking into the eyes of Jesus and seeing what He sees about you and the world around you.

REST & REFRESH

There remains therefore a rest for the people of God. For he who has entered His rest has himself also ceased from his works as God did from His. Let us therefore be diligent to enter that rest (Hebrews 4:9-11).

The unfortunate thing about rest is that we delay it so much, and almost feel guilty when we do need to rest, that we end up sabotaging our soul to the point that we end up in a major crisis we could have avoided in the first place. Rest was the first thing Adam and Eve did after being made out of dirt. Mankind was created on the sixth day after all other creation. God needed someone to take care of the creation into which He put all this time. You would have thought after God created Adam and Eve that He would have said to them, "Okay guys, let's get to work!" No, instead He creates them to enter into the seventh day, which is a day of rest.

> *Thus the heavens and the earth, and all the host of them, were finished. And on the seventh day God ended His work which He had done, and He rested on the seventh day from all His work which He had done. Then God blessed the seventh day and sanctified it, because in it He rested from all His work which God had created and made* (Genesis 2:1-3).

The first experience man had with God was a day of rest. Man was created on the sixth day, and before He can get out there to do all that He was created to do man first had to learn how to *be*. In the order of creation for man, being comes before doing. The secret of humanity reveals to us what we were first created to do—to be in the presence of God, enjoying rest with Him. He now says to us, *"Let us therefore be diligent to enter that rest"* (Heb. 4:11), or in my own words, "Don't be lazy about rest!"

While we might think that we can delay rest for a vacation time or some other time in life, we are robbing our soul until we are bankrupt in our emotional capacity. We end up on family vacation, but no one in the family is enjoying it! How did this happen? We became lazy about rest. We did not make it a fundamental part of our day, our week, our year. From the beginning, God rested on the seventh day, and then He commanded His people to take a day of rest. Even every seventh year they were to let the ground rest and take some time off for a jubilee year. Every fifty years they were commanded by God to celebrate a grand jubilee. The Spirit of God knew they still were going to need provision in those years, so what did He do? He gave them bumper crop years preceding the years of jubilee so that they could have more than enough to rest in all that God had for them during the time of rest.

My wife and I pastored a church in the greater Philadelphia area for six years. It was in the sixth year that God started speaking to me about the rest into which He wanted to bring us. I was ministering to two church campuses we had started and on top of that traveling and speaking at various conferences and events. I knew very little about rest. The unfortunate thing was, my capacity to see in the spirit, dream, and have vision for the future was so diminished I began to wonder if God was still speaking to me. Ignoring all that, I kept going and going and going. When God finally did speak to us, He told us it was time to move out of pastoring and into a place where He would give us our next assignment. It took me until the end of that year to process what God was speaking because I had no vision in my life due to a lack of rest. I finally gave in and handed the church over to our team. Moving on was incredibly difficult for me, but I knew deep in my spirit I had to trust God and get into a place where I could hear Him again.

We left from there and headed down south. When we came there, I was just learning the power of this secret. I was praying, "OK, Jesus! Show me my commission in this season. I am ready!" Excited to build something new with Him, I could not wait to hear what He was going to do with me in this new adventure. My family and I found a nice house, and we settled in, waiting for God to show us the glorious things we were going to accomplish while there. He came to me in a dream. I could feel His presence and knew we were in the dream together, and He spoke, "The only thing I want you to do here [for the land] is to mow your grass." I woke up out of the dream, trying to spiritualize everything He spoke, but I could not get past it. He did not want me to build another ministry into the land; He simply wanted me to learn rest and maintain what He had planted in that land—my front yard! Now that sounds like something relieving, but as someone who has run around more as a "human doer" than a human being it was difficult to process.

BELONGING & BELIEVING

What does rest look like? First it looks like belonging, and second it looks like believing. Out of the place of belonging we begin to experience an emergence of faith. Belonging gives us a sense that we are home with God. I travel quite a bit and have slept in some of the most comfortable hotel beds, but I can tell you for sure that there is nothing like home. I would rather sleep on the couch in my home (though my wife wouldn't let that happen) than sleep on a bed in a hotel! Home is the place of belonging. It gives us the safety to relax in a way that we could not do in a hotel or even someone else's home. Belonging is what we experience first and foremost when we come to God with our humanity. We experience a life-changing acceptance that brings us so close to our true self that it inspires us to believe and hope.

Before all else, we start out life as human beings. When our kids came into our life, there was literally nothing else they could do other than eat, poop, and sleep. I remember looking at my little baby girl with so much joy in my heart. More than anything else, I was determined to be the first, between me and Emily, to put a smile on her face. I would make crazy dad faces at her just to see her smile! Trying to get her attention, I would give her the most ridiculous faces in hopes of seeing her light up with a look that said, "You are so funny, Daddy! I love you too!" Truth be told, I was probably doing all this more for me than for her. I of course wanted her to smile, but it felt more like a sacred challenge that only someone with my special ability to make people smile could make happen. I was funny, I could do this! When she finally did crack a smile, I was so overexcited that I yelled out to Emily, "Emily, quick! Come see this! Our girl is smiling! I made her smile!" When my wife came over, she looked at me and then looked closely at her, only to reveal, "She is not smiling, babe. She is working on a special batch of brownies for her diaper, and that is the face she makes when she does that." She was right! There is absolutely nothing a little baby does functionally other than simply being adorably human.

Being is about taking a moment to be in His presence from a place of either believing or belonging. Believing and belonging are the two ways of being in God's presence. If we are connecting to His presence in believing, we are responding to who He is in us. If we are connecting to God's presence in belonging, we are responding to who we are in Him. This is an opportunity to respond to how you are connecting with God. As we rest in His presence, we are letting something very special happen. In this place, our being becomes belonging and our belonging becomes believing.

Something happens to our soul as we rest in Him. Our soul recharges, and our emotional connection to Him, ourselves, and the world around us becomes healthy again. We recharge and refresh.

BORN OF WATER

Jesus answered, "Most assuredly, I say to you, unless one is born of water and the Spirit, he cannot enter the kingdom of God" (John 3:5).

Jesus came to bring the Kingdom of God. His first public message was *"Repent, for the kingdom of heaven is at hand"* (Matt. 4:17). In Jesus' message to a religious leader named Nicodemus, He reveals that you must be born of water and Spirit to enter the Kingdom (see John 3:5). These two requirements make us fully human again. To be born of water is the physical birth that each of us had when we were delivered out of our mothers into this world. To be born of Spirit is the rebirth we have as we are born in God in heavenly places. It is the inner birth of our spirit. Our spirit, which once was dead because of sin, is now reborn because sin is taken away in Jesus, and now we are a new creation from the inside out.

Being born of water and Spirit means we are not only born to live supernaturally in the spirit as spiritual beings, but also that we are born again to live supernaturally as human beings. This incredible secret does something for us. It embraces the full reality of what Adam and Eve had in the Garden. Just as Jesus is fully God and fully man, in Christ we are fully alive in the spirit while getting to live out this wonderful thing called humanity.

GROUNDED

The secret of humanity helps to ground us. It does not run from the fact that we live on this earth, nor does it try to escape to Heaven. It embraces that fact and gives us the ability to be grounded and present with the world around us. If the goal is *on earth as it is in heaven*," then we need to come to a better understanding of our life here (Matt. 6:10). While being grounded may sound contradictory to the lifestyle of a seer, every seer needs some normal in their life to help bring them back to "planet Earth" in order for them to be present. When we embrace the secret of humanity, we grow in our relatability with other people and are able to grow in a healthier way—not away from the community of people God has put in our life, but toward a greater sense of community with the people around us. Look at Jesus.

SECRETS OF THE SEER

And Jesus increased in wisdom and stature, and in favor with God and men (Luke 2:52).

While Jesus had the ability to reveal the mysteries of the universe to the world around Him, He also had to grow in wisdom and stature as a human being. His favor was not only with God, but He had a credibility with people around Him. They could see His reliability, His dependability. This ability to embrace His humanity did not take away from His divinity; it only gave Him greater credibility when it was His time to reveal the supernatural side of His life. Even at the resurrection of Lazarus, where Jesus raised His friend from the dead, we find Him so present with people around Him, so in the moment, that it tells us, *"Jesus wept"* (John 11:35). It tells us those around Him saw Him weeping and they said, *"See how He loved him!"* (John 11:36). We know the rest of the story, which goes on to tell us the most powerful command Jesus ever declared over someone: "Lazarus, come forth!" (John 11:43). If I was coaching Jesus through this moment, I might have found myself saying, "Come on, Jesus, stop Your crying. We know what You can do! Raise the man from the dead!" I am sure I would have gotten into the same trouble Peter kept getting into when he opened his big mouth. The thing is, we see Jesus being fully present, able to weep with those who weep and rejoice with those who rejoice.

Being grounded does not stop the power of God from flowing in our life; it only enhances it. It is like the ground wire on an electric cord. The ground keeps the surges of power from ruining something that actually requires electrical power to operate. In the same way, being grounded in our humanity with the people that love us, the friends and family we have been given, and the church family of which we are a part—these things keep us grounded and prevent us from being overwhelmed, even by spiritual realities.

I once had a friend call me and ask me for some advice. He was growing in the seer and prophetic gift. The nature of his call was overwhelming, and he wanted some advice on what to do in order to have breakthrough. He had a little drive ahead of him in the car, as he was traveling for work. He was shocked at the advice I gave him. Expecting me to tell him to pray harder or to do something else, my simple advice to him was to turn on the comedy channel on the radio and let himself laugh. He was stunned, but I pressed him on this. I told him, "You need a break from all this heavy prophetic stuff in your life, and you just need to be human for a moment." Now, I was not encouraging him to lose his soul in sin or go off the deep end. He simply needed to connect with normal life in a healthy way. This moment of grounding refreshed him and gave him the ability to get back at it with more energy than he had before.

Being human is not a bad thing. In fact, Jesus laid aside His divinity to embrace humanity (see Phil. 2:5-9). Being "down to earth" is not bad, and it will not compromise your Heaven-mindedness. Doing life with people you love, being real, and embracing your humanity will give you a unique ability to be present with people around you and at the same time carry God's presence.

THE WISDOM OF PLAY

I was with Him as someone He could trust. For me, every day was pure delight, as I played in His presence all the time, playing everywhere on His earth, and delighting to be with humankind (Proverbs 8:30-31 CJB).

When you say the word *play* in some Christian circles, people might mistake you for saying something more spiritual like *pray*. As unspiritual as it sounds, God created us with the intention of experiencing the incredible wonders of His creation. Play is what every child does, and if you have ever seen a little kid who has been deprived of play, you know how something festers in him, causing him to find out negative ways to blow off that steam. When I get home from a trip or from work, the first thing I do is get down on the floor with my kids. My son never gives up an opportunity to wrestle with his dad, and I have to keep one eye open because my daughter is sneaky. She will pretend she is uninterested in the tickle fest that is happening on the floor, but I know she is really waiting for the moment when I least expect it and then she'll jump on top of the pile of bodies hitting the floor. Pretty soon I am in full-on dad mode, laughing and giggling just as loud as they are. Play is what we do to keep our souls healthy. But as we get older, something changes and we turn to darker forms of excitement. An affair sounds like a thrilling fantasy, or something else catches our fixation and it seems like fun for a moment but it will drag the soul into a very dark place.

What do you do that refreshes you and is healthy for your soul? Finding a hobby might sound like the most unspiritual thing to do, but I have found that interests quickly become a place to receive revelation. I find it fitting that Jesus was also a carpenter. No doubt there were life lessons learned in the middle of a custom-built table or house. We are even told that the first to be filled with the Holy Spirit was an artisan named Bezalel (see Exod. 31:1-5). While not everyone may pick up a paint brush for payment, many can find joy and rejuvenation in creating something beautiful.

HUMANITARIAN EFFORT

The secret of humanity is the seer's secret that a seer lifestyle is not just saying, "God bless you" to those who are hungry and expecting them to encounter God in a way that will take away the hunger. Authentic seers may have their head in the clouds, their feet on the ground, and their hands willing to get in the trenches with those in need. We can pray for revival day and night, practice high-level spiritual warfare, wrestle demons, and talk with angels, but if we do not reach out in practical ways, we are missing the point. Reach out and give a helping hand to those in need. Pray for healing, and also be the shoulder for someone to lean on at the same time.

KEYS TO UNLOCKING THIS SECRET

Practice into-me-you-see.

Come to Jesus with an open heart to be seen and known by Him. Don't be afraid to reveal your heart and your desires to Him in prayer. Let Him know what is bothering you and what is exciting you. Cast your care on Him, because He cares for you. Find a place to rest in Him, and let Him speak into your inner person. Let believing and belonging be a practice you take to the Father every day.

Find joy in something nonspiritual.

Doing something seemingly nonspiritual can also be a very healthy thing. Whether it is hiking, cooking, or working with wood as a carpenter like Jesus did, a hobby will help ground you and recharge your ability to recognize when something truly is a seer moment from God. Besides, He loves to teach us His ways in these things.

Celebrate friendships.

Being with people you love is life giving. I sincerely believe Jesus enjoyed His friendships. He was not always in "seer mode." He made people laugh, and He laughed with others. Recharge with deep and healthy friendships with people who call you back to your authentic self and give you a sense of normal.

CHAPTER
7

THE SECRET OF STILLNESS

*Be still, and know that I am God; I will be exalted among
the nations, I will be exalted in the earth!*

— PSALM 46:10

We need to find God, and He cannot be found in noise and
restlessness. God is the friend of silence. See how nature—
trees, flowers, grass—grows in silence; see the stars, the
moon, and the sun, how they move in silence.... We need
silence to be able to touch souls.

— MOTHER TERESA

Sitting in silence, my mind wrestled with every racing thought. I was new to this practice, yet something was coming alive within me. I could not stop thinking about the list of to-dos running through my mind. It was the first time I could hear my thoughts this clearly, and it was like a circus had hijacked my brain! The monkey mind would take over, and it was clearly not going to give up easily! As time went on, I kept getting stronger at this practice. I sometimes could sit for up to four hours a day in perfect stillness without worrying about what I was missing out on or the things I needed to do! You might ask, "Why would you do that? That sounds crazy!" While perhaps this is out of the ordinary to our modern-day microwave society, this secret has been at the core of every true seer's practice.

I would sit, waiting with intention and the expectation that at some point during the quiet I would experience an encounter with the living God in the seer realm. Months passed as I waited in the secret place; my spirit was growing stronger, and I could sense something unusual was about to break open.

It was in the seventh month of waiting that I discovered something. I had been waiting in quiet mostly during the day and sometimes at night. I had become so hungry for a move of God in the secret place of my prayer life that I would wait and wait and wait, but it was as if I had plateaued. I was as determined as ever to go deeper and break through into the realm of the spirit. I wanted to experience what John the revelator had encountered in the Book of Revelation: *"I was in the Spirit on the Lord's Day, and I heard behind me a loud voice, as of a trumpet"* (Rev. 1:10). As I pressed in, I realized the power of the seventh secret—**the secret of stillness**. I had been waiting on God—waiting and waiting and waiting—but I had never understood the secret of stillness in my waiting. It was like I had stumbled on this secret by accident.

One night, I was determined to experience the manifest presence of God in a way I had yet to encounter. I woke up, splashed some cold water on my face, and sat down on my bed, speaking out to God, "Alright, this is it. I am going to sit here in stillness until You come!" I sat in perfect stillness. My mind raced with random thoughts for the first 20 minutes. I would have never thought I had that level of ADD until waiting on God in stillness; the struggle is real. As I sat there in stillness, I remained calm externally until all the inner noise finally came to an end. It took some time, but it was like I had exhausted the inner circus and all those noisy thoughts finally gave up. After about 45 minutes of perfect stillness, something happened. Have you ever been so still that you can hear your own heart beating and maybe even feel it gently pumping? It was like that, but instead of my heart, I was aware of my spirit man. John says he was *in the Spirit on the Lord's day*" (Rev. 1:10), and I too could say that "I was in the Spirit" after discovering the secret of stillness.

In photography, there is a unique and lifelike way of capturing an image. It helps the viewer understand the focal point of the image by using what is called "depth of field." With depth of field, what is in focus in the image is the photograph's main subject and what is out of focus, or blurry, is the background. This helps the picture show the focal point in a more pronounced way. Often the natural is what is in focus for most of our life, with the spirit world and spiritual realities in the background—still there but just out of focus. At that moment, the focus in my awareness changed. It was as if I was seeing the spiritual world in focus and the natural world blurred in the background.

For the next few months I continued to practice the secret of stillness, and every night something happened that helped me see the realm of the spirit a little clearer and with a lot more focus. I was experiencing heavenly things like trances and visions, angelic encounters, and, more importantly, encounters with Jesus.

In the secret of stillness, we begin to unlock the intensity of hearing and seeing. Stillness gives us the ability to hear and see what is often missed when other competing noises are louder. As we dial down, we can enter by faith into the unseen realities in Christ, and our focus gives us a greater grace to receive. When we do receive, there are multiple types of encounters that are preferred types of communication from the Holy Spirit. He has spoken to mankind for thousands upon thousands of years using these methods of revelation. When we understand these ways of God, we can pay closer attention when they are happening. The secret of stillness puts us in a place to receive in these ways, the same way that sleeping puts us in a place to receive dreams from Heaven. Let's explore the various methods God uses to speak to us in the secret of stillness.

THE VOICE

In returning and rest you shall be saved; in quietness and confidence shall be your strength (Isaiah 30:15).

The other thing that happens to us as we embrace moments of stillness is that we begin to hear the voice of God clearly. Stillness is like a pair of noise-cancelling headphones. It quiets out everything else and prevents anything from stealing our attention, giving us the ability to calmly enter into a place of connection with the voice of our God.

Contrary to popular belief, the voice of God is not a loud booming voice. The voice is a much softer, gentler voice. There was a moment when even Elijah the prophet had to learn this about the voice. He had become familiar with high-intensity, powerful moments in God, yet when God comes to speak to him, something unfamiliar happens:

Then He said, "Go out, and stand on the mountain before the Lord." And behold, the Lord passed by, and a great and strong wind tore into the mountains and broke the rocks in *pieces before the Lord, but the Lord was not in the wind; and after the wind an earthquake, but the Lord was not in the earthquake; and after the earthquake a fire, but the Lord was not in the fire; and after the fire a **still small voice**. So it was, when Elijah heard it, that he wrapped his face in his mantle and went out and stood in the entrance of the cave. Suddenly a voice came to him, and said, "What are you doing here, Elijah?"* (1 Kings 19:11-13)

The great misunderstanding about God's voice, propagated by popular culture, is that He speaks big, loud, and proud. Popular culture has ingrained in us images of the iconic type of characteristics we have all come to expect. Picture a big booming voice speaking over Charlton Heston as Moses. This may well be valid, yet even Elijah had to learn that God's voice does not come in one size only. It can be big, but it also can be still and small. His audible voice can come multiple ways, and that is the reason why the seventh secret, the secret of stillness, is so profound. It gives us the ability to hear His voice in the many ways that it can come.

THE INTERNAL VOICE

Everyone has an internal voice to which we listen. We are hardwired by our Creator to hear the invisible voices. The trouble is, they can often be so subtle that we might mistake them for our own thoughts or ideas. The internal voice of God is softer than any other voice. There are times when it is clear and prominent, yet for the most part the internal voice carries a quiet confidence that offers internal strength to the listener. The psalmist would say it like this: *"I will bless the Lord who has given me counsel; my heart also instructs me in the night seasons"* (Ps. 16:7). As we listen to the voice speak to our spirit, it is like receiving instruction in our core being. It impacts us in a place nothing else can reach.

Practicing the secret of stillness will help us hear clearly the internal voice. Every seer must also learn to be an equally good hearer. Utilizing both our eyes and ears will help us be good receivers of all that the Father has for us.

Sorting through the internal voice is kind of like sorting through our own thoughts. It may not come line upon line like computer code. What I find is that the internal voice comes more like a compass than code. It is a voice that speaks faith to our heart and helps us to believe greater things about who God is and what He is doing. Leaning into His voice gives us a sense of "true north" and helps to establish us in the hope of greater things to come.

THE EXTERNAL VOICE

The secret of stillness also helps us to hear clearly those times when the audible voice of our Father wants to speak. The difficulty with the audible voice is that not everyone recognizes the source when we are hearing.

> *"Now My soul is troubled, and what shall I say? 'Father, save Me from this hour'? But for this purpose I came to this hour. Father, glorify Your name." Then a voice came from heaven, saying, "I have both glorified it and will glorify it again."* **Therefore the people who stood by and heard it said that it had thundered. Others said, "An angel has spoken to Him."** *Jesus answered and said, "This voice did not come because of Me, but for your sake"* (John 12:27-30).

What amazes me about the text above is that although they were graced to hear the external voice of God, they did not recognize it as the voice of the Father. Jesus even says, "This voice did not come because of Me, but for your sake"—as in, "I didn't need this, but you did!" Hearing God's external voice gives us an ability to believe bigger things about Him and even to see Him more clearly. When we are confronted with the difficulty of whether or not the voice we are hearing is God or something else, this is actually a good problem to have. It forces us to search out what we do and do not know about God's nature, and when we do that we are able to see Him clearly.

DAYDREAMING

Daydreaming is something that happens mostly by accident. We catch ourselves daydreaming and stop midway through like we were doing something out of character. We snap back into reality and go about our day, trying to ignore our sudden lapse of focus. This may sound like grown-up wisdom, but the problem is that it hinders us from hearing God in the daydream. The daydreamer Daniel said it like this: *"I saw in the visions of my head while on my bed, and there was a watcher, a holy one, coming down from heaven"* (Dan. 4:13). Daniel was daydreaming visions in his head. We might think daydreams are the monkey mind wandering and giving us a slight bit of entertainment, but there are more times than we realize that our daydreaming may actually be the voice of Heaven communicating something to us.

The secret of stillness intentionally puts us in a place to daydream. When quiet and not moving, we catch daydreams like we are catching great ideas passing through our mind. Being still enough to let them happen may require practice, but like any muscle, the strength for this practice grows with grace and effort.

TRANCES

Trances are an occurrence with this secret. While dreams occur when we are asleep, trances are like dreams; yet instead of being completely asleep and dreaming, our mind is alert as if we are awake while our bodies are turned off. The most common low-level form of a trance happens quite often in everyday life. We get in a car, drive down a road, and somewhere along the journey we snap back into being present and realize that we were on autopilot, driving a car! Scary, right? Hopefully for you this does not sound like a familiar scenario.

The apostle Peter was known to fall into a trance, and this experience was the very thing that opened the message of Jesus to go beyond the Jewish people only and into the hearts of Gentile nations. While Peter was waiting for dinner to be made ready, God took a moment of Peter's time and revealed to him the new plan in the unveiling of the New Covenant. The Good News at that time was being preached, but the doors for the Gospel were about to embrace all nations.

> *The next day, as they went on their journey and drew near the city, Peter went up on the housetop to pray, about the sixth hour. Then he became very hungry and wanted to eat; but while they made ready, **he fell into a trance and saw heaven opened** and an object like a great sheet bound at the four corners, descending to him and let down to the earth. In it were all kinds of four-footed animals of the earth, wild beasts, creeping things, and birds of the air. And a voice came to him, "Rise, Peter; kill and eat." But Peter said, "Not so, Lord! For I have never eaten anything common or unclean." And a voice spoke to him again the second time, "What God has cleansed you must not call common." This was done three times. And the object was taken up into heaven again (Acts 10:9-16).*

It is interesting here that within the trance, Peter sees something beyond his understanding. It should not go unnoticed that Peter even refuses to receive the message that is being shared with him. Trances have an ability to convey something to us that goes above our paradigm—something we may have never thought of before. When a trance happens at this level, it is a move of the Spirit of God. He wants undivided attention, and so He uses a trance to get us in absolute focus to convey a message that we might miss any other way. The secret of stillness sets us up for this type of encounter, and trances can become a way the Holy Spirit can communicate to us. Ezekiel, a prophet of the Mosaic Covenant, tells us of a time when the Spirit of God came upon him and he too fell into a trance:

> And it came to pass in the sixth year, in the sixth month, on the fifth day of the month, as I sat in my house with the elders of Judah sitting before me, that the hand of the Lord God fell upon me there. Then I looked, and there was a likeness, like the appearance of fire—from the appearance of His waist and downward, fire; and from His waist and upward, like the appearance of brightness, like the color of amber. He stretched out the form of a hand, and took me by a lock of my hair; and the Spirit lifted me up between earth and heaven, and brought me in visions of God to Jerusalem, to the door of the north gate of the inner court, where the seat of the image of jealousy was, which provokes to jealousy. And behold, the glory of the God of Israel was there, like the vision that I saw in the plain (Ezekiel 8:1-4).

Minding his own business while he was sitting with the elders of his tribe, Ezekiel fell into a trance. In this ecstatic experience, he was able to see what no one else saw—visions of God. Although he was there in the physical with the elders of Judah, the trance had taken him beyond his own understanding and into a realm of the supernatural to experience heavenly realities.

My first encounter with trances was not intentional on my part. It was a sovereign move of the Holy Spirit whereby I was brought into a different place beyond our physical world. Much like Ezekiel in the passage above, I saw things that were beyond my understanding. What I can tell you is that trances are not something into which you hype yourself. They happen more relationally as we connect with the Spirit of God. They are not something we sort of try to manufacture—as in, stillness + focus on God's presence = trances. No! This type of thinking is less faith based and more formulaic. Authentic faith is relational, and all the encounters we have with God are either from relationship or unto relationship.

KEYS TO THE VOICE

1. Write it down.

Then the Lord answered me and said: "Write the vision and make it plain on tablets, that he may run who reads it" (Habakkuk 2:2).

Take a moment to write down what the internal voice of God is speaking. Carefully putting on paper what God is speaking to us brings things from seeing to hearing. Taking it from hearing in your heart to seeing it on paper will breathe life to it and is the first step in making the invisible become visible.

2. Celebrate the words.

Your words were found, and I ate them, and Your word was to me the joy and rejoicing of my heart; for I am called by Your name, O Lord God of hosts (Jeremiah 15:16).

Take time to celebrate the words as though you were getting a feast. Make a big deal internally about everything that you hear from Heaven. Rejoice in it, and it will bring transformation to the profound understanding of who you are in God's heart.

3. Compare with Scripture.

> In the first year of his reign, I, Daniel, understood from the Scriptures, according to the word of the Lord given to Jeremiah the prophet, that the desolation of Jerusalem would last seventy years (Daniel 9:2 NIV).

By taking what we see and hear in the secret of stillness and comparing it to Scripture, we will grow in deeper understanding. There may be parabolic revelation that needs solid interpretation. The Scriptures are generous with examples of the language of Heaven. As we study the Scriptures, we take what is being revealed and compare it to Heaven's language already laid out in the Word. There will be some things that we hear that may be hard to understand, but the good news is that there are already plenty of examples within the Scripture that will give us understanding of what is being spoken to us.

PRACTICING STILLNESS

> But those who wait on the Lord shall renew their strength; they shall mount up with wings like eagles, they shall run and not be weary, they shall walk and not faint (Isaiah 40:31).

Practicing stillness is a lost art that is being recaptured as a fundamental part of our faith walk. Some have called this "waiting on God," but waiting on God can be misunderstood as something else. Often when we throw out the phrase "waiting on God" people assume that means we are patiently waiting for God to do something while going about our daily life. This may be true, but the deeper level of waiting on God is about practicing stillness in order to embrace an encounter. What I am about to share with you about the secret of stillness has activated a level of visitations from God that everyone may experience. If they learn the secret of stillness and wait with their whole heart, soul, and body still, they will encounter realms of God's presence in heavenly proportions.

1. Find a quiet place.

The biggest distraction to the secret of stillness will be environmental. Are you attempting to practice this secret in the middle of the day in your living room where your family is most active? If so, you are going to set yourself up for failure. Find a solid place of quiet to step into this secret. The Scriptures call this sacred space "the secret place."

> He who dwells in the **secret place** of the Most High shall abide under the shadow of the Almighty (Psalm 91:1).

The secret place is the space we have in our pursuit of God's presence where we can find no distraction. What is the litmus test for something being a secret place? Well, this holy space is free of distractions (both good and bad); it is free from social media, free from noise disturbances, and free from anything than else that can keep us from being able to practice the secret of stillness. Finding this space may be a chore at first because you may think you are in a secret place, but what if something or someone finds out that you are there? Years ago, there was a space that I initially thought might be a secret place for me to practice the secret of stillness. Unfortunately, a mocking bird also thought this was a safe place for him to make his calls all day and night, right outside the window of the room I was in. My frustration grew until I was praying for God to move the bird or perhaps do something worse to it! I then had to relocate the secret place to engage God in stillness. It was a chore, but I finally found a place to practice.

2. *Timing is everything.*

The secret of stillness is best practiced at the right time of day, and what that time is depends on the person's lifestyle, work, family life, etc. For instance, I know that I am unable to best practice the secret of stillness when I first wake up. My mind is way too active, and I cannot seem to engage in absolute stillness at that time. I want to accomplish something, whether it is drink a cup of coffee, suit up for the day, make the kids breakfast, talk to my wife, etc. This time of day is difficult for me to practice stillness. I have also discovered that around 2:00 or 3:00 in the afternoon is a very good time for me. It reminds me of the time when Adam and Eve walked with God in the cool of the day.

> *And they heard the sound of the Lord God walking in the garden in the cool of the day, and Adam and his wife hid themselves from the presence of the Lord God among the trees of the garden* (Genesis 3:8).

Find the time that works best for you and the time that you find the presence of God is actually showing up to your secret place party. In one of my last books, *Supernatural Revolution*, I go through the four watches of the night. Each of these watches has a different purpose and benefit. Finding what time works for you and your schedule will be highly subjective. Jesus would retreat in the night to talk with the Father. His schedule may be different than ours. Some of us may work the night shift and need to carve out some time during the day. Everyone is different. I kept mental notes as to where and when I saw the most breakthrough. This helped me hone in on the best use of my time.

3. *Engage the presence of God.*

The secret of stillness is not about being in "timeout," away from everybody; it is about being highly engaged with the presence of God on a level beyond words. As you practice this secret, you will notice that your awareness of God's presence will expand. The beautiful mystery of God's presence inside of you will become much more real in those moments of stillness. Paul the apostle gave us a glimpse into the importance of this revelation:

> *To them God willed to make known what are the riches of the glory of this mystery among the Gentiles: which is Christ in you, the hope of glory* (Colossians 1:27).

We may be theologically aware that Christ is in us, yet this marvelous revelation is designed by Heaven to go beyond head knowledge and into heart experience. As we practice the secret of stillness, we are not just trying to attract God's presence from the outside of us; rather, we are expanding our awareness of God's presence inside of us. God's presence inside of us is called "the anointing." Christ, or Messiah, is a Greek word meaning "anointed one." The anointing is not just some wispy energy that floats around invisibly doing God's bidding. The anointing is God concentrate. Like orange juice from concentrate, God has concentrated all the best parts of His nature and put the fullness of Himself in way that can be imparted to His children. The anointing is God concentrate. It fills us and guides us into a greater encounter in the revelation of who God is. While Christ is in us, encouraging our hearts and renewing our relationship with God, the hope of glory is the aim of Christ within. This brings us to the question, what is the glory if it is the hope and aim of Christ in you? If Christ in us as God concentrate, the hope of glory is God revealed. The glory is the revelation of the fullness of God; it is the entirety of His nature, the splendor of His majesty, the total reveal of His abundant goodness and mercy. Engaging the presence of God within us takes us from glory to glory. And as the Scriptures say, *"But we all, with unveiled face, beholding as in a mirror the glory of the Lord, are being transformed into the same image from glory to glory, just as by the Spirit of the Lord"* (2 Cor. 3:18).

4. Remain calm.

Someone once said, "Peace is the soil of revelation." If peace is the soil, then anxiety is a weed. We are encouraged to great expectation, which is far different than anxiety; yet one can become a false imitator of the other. Anxiety is a form of worry for something, while faith is a state of confident expectation. Both seem to be aiming toward the same thing or often the same result, but one is founded on courage while the other is founded on fear.

> *Be anxious for nothing, but in everything by prayer and supplication, with thanksgiving, let your requests be made known to God; and the peace of God, which surpasses all understanding, will guard your hearts and minds through Christ Jesus* (Philippians 4:6-7).

One thing that I have noticed while in stillness is that there is a moment when a visitation from Heaven is about to happen and I naturally start becoming anxious. My heartbeat starts to increase and excitement levels rise, but what I have found is that remaining calm in those moments is a discipline that gives me the ability to receive.

"Letting go and letting God," as one might put it. While we can practice self-control, we cannot determine what God is going to do in our pursuit of Him. I cannot be anxious to the point that I am trying to will a visitation from God or trying to will a trance or another type of encounter. That just won't work. As we engage God and let Him do what He does best, our connectivity to His presence will increase.

Peace keeps us locked on to His presence, while anxiety shakes us from His presence. It doesn't mean He has left us or forsaken us; it simply means we have lost sight of where He is at.

I have talked to many seer-type prophetic people, and often they fall into a struggle because for a certain time period God spoke to them consistently through dreams or in another way through visions but now it is as if it has dried up. My encouragement to them remains the same: God is always moving and doing something new; perhaps focus where He is at, and stop focusing where He is not!

VISITATIONS

I will come to visions and revelations of the Lord (2 Corinthians 12:1b).

Encounters have always been a main component of being a seeker. The Scriptures themselves are a compilation of encounters that normal people had with a supernatural God. Every encounter led them to a greater understanding of the infinite goodness of God and the surpassing greatness of His Kingdom. It is no wonder he says, *"Call to Me, and I will answer you, and show you great and mighty things, which you do not know"* (Jer. 33:3). There are things yet to be discovered about God; He has not finished revealing the depths of His love and wonder. So, how do we encounter this God?

*God, who made the world and everything in it, since He is Lord of heaven and earth, does not dwell in temples made with hands. Nor is He worshiped with men's hands, as though He needed anything, since He gives to all life, breath, and all things. And He has made from one blood every nation of men to dwell on all the face of the earth, and has determined their preappointed times and the boundaries of their dwellings, **so that they should seek the Lord, in the hope***

that they might grope for Him and find Him, though He
is not far from each one of us; for in Him we live and move
and have our being, as also some of your own poets have said,
"*For we are also His offspring*" (Acts 17:24-28).

The purpose of life begins with seeking God and finding Him. He has placed every one of us in different circumstances and different cultures so that our hearts will open to seeking Him in the place we are at. The good news is He is closer than we may realize. Inside of our life circumstances, each of us has a divinely placed hunger that can only be satisfied by God's presence. Leaning into this hunger we come to the conclusion, "There must be more." That "more" is found in the discovery of God when we encounter Him. Worship begins to move us into a place of connection, and we long for Him in a way that moves His heart. The tricky part about seeking Him is that our perception of pursuing God can fall into the trap of achieving rather than receiving.

An achieving mentality is a terrible thing that happens to many of us as we begin to seek Him. We may think that God is like any other shiny object we have worked hard to attain at one point or another in our life. We may think, "I know how this works: I do this and do that, and then *bam*, I find God." The reality is, God is received, not achieved. The secret of stillness puts us in a place of absolute dependence on Him, where we trust that He is going to reveal Himself like He said He would. The secret of stillness brings us out of being a good achiever and into being a good receiver. Every seer is a good receiver, and as we increase in peace, we will find that our ability to receive is heightened and we can come into tune with Him and how He wants to encounter us.

Visitations are the result of being a good receiver. We learn to host His presence by engaging Him in the secret place. We learn to receive Him through stillness when He shows up. Being still puts us in a place of being present with God, and when we learn to be present with Him, we will encounter the presence of God.

KEYS TO UNLOCKING THIS SECRET

The secret of stillness will become the Samson strength in the seer's life. As you practice this secret, you will notice an increased awareness of the unseen realm. Things that you would not typically notice in the past will seem to be happening with more frequency. You will become more aware of the angels of God, the faith of God, and the activity of Heaven. If you guard this secret, unusual things will happen to give you a greater knowledge of God's presence in your life.

Get comfortable.

Too often I find people trying to practice this secret in the most uncomfortable positions. No need to do a lotus position—forget that. Lay down on your back on a comfy mattress. Get that lazy chair warmed up, and lie there with your inward focus aimed at Heaven. If you fall asleep in those positions, maybe you needed that and that was the visitation you needed—sleep!

Pay attention.

One of the more difficult things that will happen in an encounter is the inability to pay attention. Sometimes we can get overly excited that we are simply having an encounter and forget to pay attention to the encounter. Pay attention to the encounter when it is happening. Focus on what you are hearing, what is going on around you. If you pay attention, you will be able to retain the revelation that is being shown to you.

Start small.

Do not make the mistake of thinking you will be trying to tackle two hours of stillness your first go. Start small and do five minutes. Believe me, this first five minutes is going to feel like forever. After you tackle five minutes, move to seven and then ten. Be confident that even five minutes of stillness is still great breakthrough in your pursuit of God.

CHAPTER
8

THE SECRET OF SOUND

*The wilderness and the wasteland shall be glad for them, and
the desert shall rejoice and blossom as the rose; it shall blossom
abundantly and rejoice, even with joy and singing. The glory
of Lebanon shall be given to it, the excellence of Carmel and
Sharon. They shall see the glory of the Lord, the excellency of
our God.*

— ISAIAH 35:1-2

Music is the mediator between the life of the senses and
the life of the spirit.

— BEETHOVEN

One morning while between sleep and consciousness I could hear it. Somewhere in the twilight of the morning I found my mind alert, but it was as if my body was still asleep. The most beautiful sound was echoing throughout the room as if a full-on symphonic orchestra had taken over the airwaves and was now playing something heavenly. The sound was coursing through me as if it were a wave catching me up into it. And in a moment, it stopped. I was now fully awake. I could still recall the notes, my spirit alive within me as if I had just stepped out of a concert filled with the most moving sounds. I realized I was hearing the sounds of Heaven.

I am convinced that Heaven is filled with the most glorious sounds and that the interaction between sound, light, life, and the movement of Heaven will completely astound us for all of eternity. Listening to those sounds immersed me in something that I believe has the power to wake up even the most dead in spirit.

It was as if that music had marked my soul. Deep within me a new hunger had formed, and it was to hear the song I heard playing in that place between Heaven and earth. I ran to every music store, testing out everything from Gregorian monks to more instrumental tracks. I finally landed on Handel's *Messiah*. This was something different, but it sounded most like the song I had heard. I took it home and played it in my bedroom, immersing myself in every note. It was in those moments I discovered the power of the eighth secret—**the secret of sound**.

With each wave of music playing over and over, it was like the music itself was peeling back my eyes to see the unseen. My spirit was so affected by the sound that I put the album on repeat for the next year and did not change it to anything else. Every time I entered that room, it was a sanctuary that I knew I could go to and enter into the presence of God with ease. My dream life skyrocketed and vision increased. This incredible discovery was accelerating my spirit into seer encounters and giving me a hunger for more.

SOUNDS OF HEALING

Sound has a way of unlocking supernatural realities in each of us. There has always been a partnership between sound and the prophetic spirit. Seer encounters are opened up when heavenly songs are played. We can see this even in the ancient practices of the prophetic. Samuel the seer tells King Saul of a traveling band of musicians playing and prophesying:

> *And it will happen, when you have come there to the city, that you will meet a group of prophets coming down from the high place with a stringed instrument, a tambourine, a flute, and a harp before them; and they will be prophesying. Then the Spirit of the Lord will come upon you, and you will prophesy with them and be turned into another man* (1 Samuel 10:5b-6).

The convergence of sound and the supernatural is evident. Something is awakened even within Saul, and he too will step into the prophetic spirit, prophesy, and be transformed to take on his destiny as the anointed king over Israel. Sound has the ability to usher us into encounters with God and the supernatural and bring us to a place to see beyond the seen into the unseen world of possibility and the miraculous.

The study of sound's effect on the brain gives us insight into its potential power. One such study did A/B testing on patients about to undergo surgery. One group was given anti-anxiety drugs, while the other participants were randomly given music to listen to instead of drugs. During this study, scientists monitored the stress levels of patients as well as the levels of the stress-related hormone cortisol. The fascinating results came back: between those who had taken anti-anxiety medication and those who had listened to music, the clear winner in lower stress and lower cortisol levels were those listening to music.[14] Dr. Levitin, who published the research in the journal *Trends in Cognitive Sciences*, stated, "The promise here is that music is arguably less expensive than drugs, and it's easier on the body and it doesn't have side effects."[15]

> *Sound has been used for centuries as a way of calming the body and bringing people into a right frame of mind. King Saul in his later years would deal with a high level of insanity. When the yet-to-be king, David, enters the story, we find him soothing Saul with songs, helping him come back to his right mind: "And so it was, whenever the spirit from God was upon Saul, that David would take a harp and play it with his hand. Then Saul would become refreshed and well, and the distressing spirit would depart from him"* (1 Samuel 16:23).

The secret of sound brings us back to the healing roots of music. It is seeing music not just as entertainment, but as a means of stepping into a place of healing where the Spirit of God can minister to us in a deep way.

Hearing to See

There is an incredibly touching story of Daniel Kish, whose eyes were removed before the age of 13 months because of retinal cancer. Without the use of his natural sight, Daniel developed a method of seeing that is typically used in bats, a few bird species, dolphins, and some other swimming mammals. This unique ability is called echo-location. Echolocation is the unique use of reflected sound waves to locate objects in the surrounding environment.

When I was a kid growing up in St. Louis, we had bats that would come out at night, hoping to find their next bug meal. Swooping up and down in the air, they were looking for anything their echolocation abilities picked up. As an experiment, my father would show us just how accurate they were in this skill. Throwing a tennis ball up in the sky, we would watch a bat swoop in, chasing it almost the entire way back down to the ground, while my dad explained the science behind the whole event.

Daniel Kish had developed the same thing. He was able to hear the sound waves crashing in on objects around him, giving him the ability to live life with a level of freedom that others with eyes experience. As he explains, *"That clicking sound bounces off surfaces throughout the environment... And it comes back with information—distances, locations, positions, contours, densities. I can construct images from that information."*[16]

Sound had given Daniel the ability to see in a way that others did not know was possible. By age six, Daniel was riding a bike and doing the things that other boys his age were doing. Intrigued by the unique ability Daniel possessed, neuroscientists studied Daniel and discovered that when he clicks, he activates the visual part of his brain.

The secret of sound unlocks the mystery that there are ways to see in the spirit that are not discovered with our eyes, but our ears. When we activate this secret, sound illuminates the imagination with the ability to see the unseen with a different set of eyes. As with Daniel Kish, sound activates the visual part of your brain—but to see by faith what the Father wants to show you. I notice that my ability to see in the spirit increases exponentially when I worship and listen to certain musical notes. It is as if those notes light up the unseen world around me and the sound waves bounce off unseen realities, with my spirit catching the feedback of those things. The secret of sound illuminates our spirit to hear in a greater capacity, giving us a different type of sight for the invisible realities of God.

WORSHIP IN SPIRIT

As we read through the examples in Scripture, it is safe to say that worship is a fundamental activity in Heaven. The sounds of Heaven are constant, as those around the throne are reciting the unending glories of the one on the throne. The four living creatures around the throne initiating the worship experience are backed up by the 24 elders, who echo their praise to the Creator.

> *The four living creatures, each having six wings, were full of eyes around and within. And they do not rest day or night, saying: "Holy, holy, holy, Lord God Almighty, who was and is and is to come!" Whenever the living creatures give glory and honor and thanks to Him who sits on the throne, who lives forever and ever, the twenty-four elders fall down before Him who sits on the throne and worship Him who lives forever and ever, and cast their crowns before the throne, saying: "You are worthy, O Lord, To receive glory and honor and power; for You created all things, and by Your will they exist and were created"* (Revelation 4:8-11).

Soundwaves of worship fill the atmosphere, and those who worship do not seem to grow tired of the joy and celebration of bragging upon the one on the throne. This supernatural scene is the hope we look forward to, knowing that we will one day join in this celebration in heavenly places.

While this has been going on in Heaven for eons, mankind has looked for a location to worship. Buildings, spaces, and places deemed holy sites, set apart for sacred purposes, give us permission to worship and encounter the living God. Jesus lived in a time of tension where one person supported one location of worship and another person had a different idea. In His travels, Jesus runs across a Samaritan woman who is mystified by the worship culture of her day. Where will she worship is the burning question on her heart.

> *"Our fathers worshiped on this mountain, and you Jews say that in Jerusalem is the place where one ought to worship." Jesus said to her, "Woman, believe Me, the hour is coming when you will neither on this mountain, nor in Jerusalem, worship the Father. You worship what you do not know; we know what we worship, for salvation is of the Jews. But the hour is coming, and now is, when the true worshipers will worship the Father in spirit and truth; for the Father is seeking such to worship Him. God is Spirit, and those who worship Him must worship in spirit and truth"* (John 4:20-24).

While the Jews worshiped in one place and the Samaritans in another, the great reveal to the Samaritan woman is that God is Spirit, and because He is Spirit, true worship will one day take place in spirit and truth. The big controversy here is the issue of location. Where should we worship, and in what way? Jesus answers the who, the where, and the how: *"God is Spirit* [who], *and those who worship Him must worship in spirit* [where] *and truth* [how]" (John 4:24). The issue of location is settled—not on this mountain or another; rather, worshipers who live out the reality of the truth Jesus is revealing will go beyond the physical locations of this world and into the spirit to worship God, who is Spirit. The secret of sound reveals to us that worship transports us by faith into the spirit realm to worship God. He is not bound by a place, a location, a building, or an element. God

The Secret of Sound

is Spirit, and He seeks worshipers who will join Him in the spirit for worship.

This is the reason why, although we may not physically be at our favorite worship event, when we tune in through live streaming we are able to enter in as if we are there. Whether it is live streaming or recorded live, we can worship as if we were there and it transports us to the same place in the spirit that sound took God's people!

SOUND ACTIVATED

"But now bring me a musician." Then it happened, when the musician played, that the hand of the Lord came upon him (2 Kings 3:15).

The secret of the seer is that they are *sound activated.* Music gives the seer the ease of entering into the prophetic nature of God. When the Spirit of God comes upon them, the flow and the ease of God's grace comes as well, activating the ability to see and hear the activity of Heaven. Eyes begin to open to the realm of the spirit, and the flow of understanding is increased. Supernatural gifts are activated, and we can step into a place of fellowship with the Spirit of Creativity. The secret of sound acts like a spark plug, helping us step into realms of the supernatural that we might struggle to get to on our own. It puts us in a mood to receive and gives us a calm in our spirit to enter in by peace to the ways of God. Simple tones and sounds increase our awareness of His presence and bring a heightened state of memory recall, giving us the ability to remember accurately what God is revealing.

University students have been using this secret for years. We have all heard during finals week that we should play some classical music to bring out the best of our test-taking abilities. Is it true: Are our studies enhanced while listening to Mozart, Bach, or Brahms?

Researchers in France published the results of their study in *Learning and Individual Differences*: Two groups of students taking the same quiz were studied in an attempt to discern the difference between those who listened to classical music and those that did not while listening to the same lecture. The quiz given on the lecture material showed that those who listened to classical music scored higher than those who did not. Researchers could only guess that those who listened to classical music were more receptive to the information they were receiving because of the heightened emotional state they were in from the music.[17] To me, this revealed that intelligence is not the absence of emotions but the healthy activity of emotions that bring us into a higher place of receptivity.

The secret of sound takes us into a frame of mind to receive and be moved by what we are seeing. Think about some of your favorite films. We may not have noticed, but during the most moving moments, the music sets the tone for us to really believe and enter into what we are watching. In the same way, using music to increase connection with God takes us into a deeper place of being present with Him and opens our senses to receive.

In the last century, the impact of music on plant life was studied to see whether sound activated any positive effects on growth and yield. Dr. T. C. Singh, head of the botany department at India's Annamalai University, conducted a series of studies researching plant yield and growth when listening to classical music. It was discovered that balsam plants grew 20 percent in height and the overall biomass saw an increase of 72 percent when classical music was played in their environment. Dr. Singh also discovered that seeds that were exposed to the same music had something remarkable happen to them as they were planted and grown: not only was the size difference evident, but they produced more leaves and showed greater aesthetic qualities than the others.[18]

In the grapevine region of Montalcino in Tuscany, grape grower Giancarlo Cignozzi has a special section of his vineyard wherein classical music is played over the vines. The result, he says, is that it causes the grapes to be more robust and the sugar content to be richer in those grapes that are closer to the speakers. The audiophiles over at Bose, the maker of ultra high-definition speakers, took an interest in the winemaker and even donated 72 speakers and financed increased research.[19]

Keys to Unlocking This Secret

Some might call this emotionalism and challenge this as nothing more than feelings and hype. While I don't doubt this can happen, we should not be so naïve as to throw the good out with the bad. Here are some simple steps to activate this secret:

Find your sound.

There are certain sounds that I have come to discover can activate this secret. Find your sound and what brings you into the place of encounter. For me, Alberto and Kimberly Rivera have an amazing sound that takes me into a place of seeing, hearing, and dreaming. Several of their songs are on my go-to playlist that I play when I am meditating on God's Word, soaking, or simply sleeping. Find your sound.

Avoid the noise.

When I first started practicing the secret of sound, I found incredible music that would take me right into encounters but just as soon pull me right out. I could not figure out how this was happening. I realized that the music I was listening to would throw in a loud crashing cymbal every once in a while just to keep it interesting. Maybe they did that so the listener would stay alert while listening and not veer off the road into some ditch. I get it. What I have found, though, is that those sounds are often just noise. Noise is unwanted sound. It keep us from entering in and enjoying where the Holy Spirit wants to take us in that moment. Avoid the noise.

Play when sleeping.

The secret of sound can also be used when sleeping. This is not a time to put on your big band music or electronica. This is a time when you put on something that keeps you sleeping but sets the mood for the Spirit of Wisdom and Revelation to fill your dream life. I find low and slow tones are often the best, as they produce a sound that is easier to receive while sleeping that won't wake you up. Play when sleeping.

CHAPTER

9

THE SECRET OF
ABUNDANCE

Warning: This mystery is not a get-rich-quick scheme or
a teaching on how God wants you to be rich. This mystery is not about money but about a lifestyle of abundance.
I encourage the reader to keep an open mind, as God *"is
able to do exceedingly abundantly above all that we ask or
think, according to the power that works in us"* (Eph. 3:20).

*And God is able to make all grace abound toward you, that
you, always having all sufficiency in all things, may have an
abundance for every good work.*
—2 CORINTHIANS 9:8

*D*uring my time as a pastor, a wonderful woman within our community came to me to tell me a story. She and her husband had been praying for God to bless her and give her a significant financial increase so that they could pay off some debt that they had, give where they wanted to, and on top of all this be blessed to take some time on a much-needed vacation. During this time, she and her husband were going through their house, getting rid of random things that were taking up space. There was a collection of art hanging in one corner of the room, all from the same artist. Some of the collection was unframed, as her husband had been given most of it as a gift for some work he had done in the past. A couple of the pieces he had paid $100 for, but for the most part the rest had been given as gifts. Unaware of how much they were worth, they kept them loosely arranged in a pile on the floor, some positioned upright between the wall and the floor.

While cleaning house, she and her husband thought they should see if any of them had any value and put one of them up for auction online. They found a live auction website for art—sort of like an eBay for fine art—and placed it there at a beginning bid of a dollar. As time went on, over a course of days they came back to see the current bid of the auction. To their shock, the current bid was roughly around $10,000 USD! It did not stop there. The auction was only halfway through, and within a couple days the final bid came in at $32,500. Ecstatic, she told me, "Jamie, we have a bunch of these just laying around the house—all from the same artist!" My encouragement to her was, "Make sure you pick the rest up off the floor!"

This fantastic story highlights the ninth secret of the seer—**the secret of abundance**. Who knows for how long these wonderful folks walked past these pieces of fine art and saw them lying on the floor but did not truly see their real value. This is the secret of abundance:

the ability to see the world around you—not just the invisible, but what is already visible, with eyes that truly see.

HIDDEN IN PLAIN SIGHT

The seer does not see only the spiritual realities, the realm of angels and demons and visions and dreams. The seer has eyes to see what is hidden in plain sight in the physical world around us. Things that others might call common, the seer sees value in—value that is not staring everyone in the face but is hidden in such a way that it takes a trained eye to see its promise and potential.

Jesus took His disciples on a little journey to show them the Kingdom. In broad daylight, He took a few small fish and seven loaves of bread and did something even the disciples could not perceive.

> *So He commanded the multitude to sit down on the ground. And He took the seven loaves and gave thanks, broke them and gave them to His disciples to set before them; and they set them before the multitude. They also had a few small fish; and having blessed them, He said to set them also before them. So they ate and were filled, and they took up seven large baskets of leftover fragments. Now those who had eaten were about four thousand. And He sent them away* (Mark 8:6-9).

With the multitude all around and the disciples at His side, Jesus multiplies the loaves and fish and creates such a feast out of something so small that they need to collect the remains as leftover pieces and put them in seven large baskets. His disciples are fed, and so is everyone else.

When they leave that place, they set sail in a boat and the most bizarre thing happens to Jesus. The religious rulers of the day, known as Pharisees, come out, *"seeking from Him a sign from heaven, testing Him"* (Mark 8:11). The wild thing to me is that Jesus had just done a sign. The problem is, they wanted a spiritual sign, but Jesus just did a natural sign. They wanted some kind of heavenly light show or maybe something more spiritual, but Jesus gave the sign of the multiplication of something earthly and natural—physical food. The problem is, they had become so spiritual that they couldn't see the physical resource right in front of them. Jesus gets into the boat again, and another interesting thing happens:

> *Now the disciples had forgotten to take bread, and they did not have more than one loaf with them in the boat* (Mark 8:14).

When I was a kid, my father would make bread on Saturdays at our house. All the way upstairs you could smell the bread being prepared. The smells were intoxicating. I joke that there is a reason Jesus was tempted by the devil with gluten. My brothers and I were all thinking the same thing: *That bread is all mine!* My dad grew up in an Italian home so bread was traditionally served with a dipping plate of olive oil and cracked black pepper over the top, with Pecorino Romano cheese. When you took a slice of that bread and dipped it into the olive oil, it was heavenly. My brothers and I all had the same thing on our mind: *Who was going to eat the bread first, and how many slices were we each going to get?* Our minds could not be distracted; our eyes were fixed on that bread. If so much as a single slice went missing, someone better have had some answers. Can you imagine the disciples sitting there in the boat with one loaf of bread between 13 grown men—one Jesus and twelve disciples? Everyone in that boat would have known where that one loaf was! Jesus was aware of the tension, and He used a physical symbol to illustrate a spiritual problem.

Then He charged them saying, "Take heed, beware of the leaven of the Pharisees and the leaven of Herod." And they reasoned among themselves, saying, "It is because we have no bread" (Mark 8:15-16).

How did they go from one loaf of bread to no loaf of bread? Where did the bread go? It was there one moment and suddenly it is gone? If one of them had eaten the loaf, surely Peter would have had something to say about it.

But Jesus, being aware of it, said to them, "Why do you reason because you have no bread? Do you not yet perceive nor understand? Is your heart still hardened? Having eyes, do you not see? And having ears, do you not hear? And do you not remember?" (Mark 8:17-18)

Jesus knows about the loaf. It is as if they cannot see the loaf hidden in plain sight. Something very spiritual is happening, and it is blocking the disciples' ability to see and hear. Why can they not see the loaf right in front of them? Where did it go? Jesus warns the disciples about *"the leaven of the Pharisees and the leaven of Herod"* (Mark 8:15). Remember the Pharisees and how spiritual they had become, but they couldn't even recognize the abundance right in front of their eyes? Jesus was working miracles all the time, but the Pharisees still could not see it. It was as if a blindness had taken over their spirits. Jesus warns about this blindness. He even mentions Herod as well— the blindness of the leaven of Herod. *"Having eyes, do you not see? And having ears, do you not hear?"* (Mark 8:18). Herod wanted to see a miracle done by Jesus as well, but Herod was just like the Pharisees (see Luke 23:8). With a *"heart still hardened,"* he avoided any transformation to the state of his heart (Mark 8:17).

The warning to beware of the leaven of the Pharisees and Herod is still just as important to us today. This type of thinking darkens our eyes and ears and keeps us from seeing abundance in the world around us. Just like the disciples, instead of a loaf of bread we see lack. Instead of the abundance of the multiplication of the loaves and fish, we cannot fully see what He has already done for us.

> *"When I broke the five loaves for the five thousand, how many baskets full of fragments did you take up?" They said to Him, "Twelve." "Also, when I broke the seven for the four thousand, how many large baskets full of fragments did you take up?" And they said, "Seven." So He said to them, "How is it you do not understand?"* (Mark 8:19-21)

Jesus asks them to take an audit of what is around them, what they witnessed with their eyes. In the same way, are you aware of the abundance that is around you?

It is amazing to me just how much we have that we cannot see. The secret of abundance gives us eyes to see the generosity of God in everyday life. It helps us to see that piece of art on the floor for its real value. It helps us to see that person in front of us on the train as a child of God and not just another passenger. It helps us to see the abundance that God is providing for us every day that may go unnoticed.

Fasting has become a way that I step into the secret of abundance. I am not fasting for things; rather, if I do fast, it is to gain clarity to see what I already have been given. It is to get eyes to see and ears to hear, along with a heart to understand. It amazes me how little food I think I have in my pantry, but as soon as I begin the fast I start seeing the incredible four-course meal waiting for me at the end of it. Suddenly, I am finding things in my fridge that I had no idea were there. The secret of abundance takes over, and I am given eyes to see what was hidden in plain sight.

TRUE VALUE

The secret of abundance gives us the ability to see true value in something. It is that perception that sees that the handcrafted wallet created by the street vendor in Mexico is worth more than the one in the glass case down the road at the nearest high-end department store. When we see the world through this lens, we can discern abundance.

I believe Jesus walked in the secret of abundance. He was able to identify true value when the woman gave an offering that was far below what everyone else gave. It was so valuable because she gave out of her lack, while others gave out of their surplus. Look at how He responds to this situation:

> *Now Jesus sat opposite the treasury and saw how the people put money into the treasury. And many who were rich put in much. Then one poor widow came and threw in two mites, which make a quadrans. So He called His disciples to Himself and said to them, "Assuredly, I say to you that this poor widow has put in more than all those who have given to the treasury; for they all put in out of their abundance, but she out of her poverty put in all that she had, her whole livelihood"* (Mark 12:41-44).

There is a story in Scripture about Jacob and his struggle to walk in the blessing of his father-in-law. He worked so hard with the intent of marrying the daughter of the man for whom he worked. When he came to the end of seven years of work, the father-in-law agreed to give his daughter's hand in marriage. The only problem is that at the end of the seven years, he pulled the veil back on their wedding night only to discover that his father-in-law conned him into marrying the wrong daughter. His vows were spoken, and now he was married to the ugly sister. More determined than ever, Jacob worked for another seven years to receive the father's blessing to remarry and this time get it right. On Jacob's way out of the father-in-law's family business, Jacob asks him for a blessing:

Let me pass through all your flock today, removing from there all the speckled and spotted sheep, and all the brown ones among the lambs, and the spotted and speckled among the goats; and these shall be my wages (Genesis 30:32).

The culture at the time of Jacob considered any speckled and spotted sheep to be reject sheep. Even though they were sheep, because they were speckled and spotted they were looked down upon in the culture. When Jacob proposed to remove the speckled and spotted sheep, his father-in-law thought it was a good deal. He was probably thinking, "Great! Take them since they are lower-class sheep!" The father-in-law agrees, and Jacob sets out on a three-day journey with his new flock. His father-in-law was about to discover that these were the stronger sheep.

Here is a great example of the secret of abundance at work. While everyone in the culture could not see the value of spotted sheep, Jacob was given a vision by God to walk into abundance by perceiving the true value of the sheep, which no one else could see. How did this happen? God gave Jacob a plan in a dream:

And it happened, at the time when the flocks conceived, that I lifted my eyes and saw in a dream, and behold, the rams which leaped upon the flocks were streaked, speckled, and gray-spotted. Then the Angel of God spoke to me in a dream, saying, "Jacob." And I said, "Here I am." And He said, "Lift your eyes now and see, all the rams which leap on the flocks are streaked, speckled, and gray-spotted; for I have seen all that Laban is doing to you. I am the God of Bethel, where you anointed the pillar and where you made a vow to Me.

Now arise, get out of this land, and return to the land of your family" (Genesis 31:10-13).

Seeing what no one else could see, Jacob created a plan to be blessed with what everyone else in that society considered worthless. *"Thus the man became exceedingly prosperous, and had large flocks, female and male servants, and camels and donkeys"* (Gen. 30:43).

KEYS TO UNLOCKING THIS SECRET

Sow where you grow.

Like any investor, gardener, or even farmer, sow where you know there is maximum growth. *"Give, and it will be given to you: good measure, pressed down, shaken together, and running over will be put into your bosom. For with the same measure that you use, it will be measured back to you"* (Luke 6:38). Unlocking abundance first begins with living a generous life. Yet even generosity is smart enough to discern what is a good place to give and what is not. Imagine God has given you a banana tree. Your responsibility is now to use the secret of abundance and maximize where this plant will thrive. Would you ever try to plant the banana tree in the desert? I don't think so. You are going to look for the right conditions: the perfect soil, the right sunlight, and the best amount of rain for a plant like that. In the same way, give your time, energy, and resources to something you know is going to give you great return on your investment.

Make wise purchases.

She considers a field and buys it; from her profits she plants a vineyard (Proverbs 31:16).

Pay personal attention to where and what you spend your resources on. The secret of abundance bears the fruit of assets, while the destruction of poverty carries the burden of liability. Everyone is going to spend money, but what are you spending yours on? Is it bringing greater freedom in your life or greater hassle? Do your homework and research the best options. This gives you the ability to discover true value and grow in the secret of abundance.

Perceive potential.

> *She perceives that her merchandise is good, and her lamp does not go out by night* (Proverbs 31:18).

If you do not understand the value of what you have, someone else will make that determination for you, and it may not be abundance. Moses had an old staff made out of wood, and God told him it was enough to deliver His people out of slavery. Have you perceived the value of what is in your possession? Ask God to give you eyes to see the potential of the things you have been given.

CHAPTER
10

THE SECRET OF WORDS

By faith we understand that the worlds were framed by the word of God, so that the things which are seen were not made of things which are visible.

—HEBREWS 11:3

Words create worlds.

—RABBI ABRAHAM HESCHEL

I was in one of my favorite places in the world, Texas. If you have not been to Texas, you have to go. Everything really is bigger there. Sometimes even God seems bigger in Texas! I had been invited to speak at a growing church. The lead pastor and her team had been believing God for breakthrough during these meetings. I had been brought in to speak life over this growing movement. Wonderful things were already happening, and it was my joy to come in and partner with the works that Jesus was already doing with them. Impressed by the Holy Spirit to share on the power of speaking life, I felt that something amazing was about to happen. I started off sharing from the Scriptures:

> *Death and life are in the power of the tongue. Those who love it will eat its fruit* (Proverbs 18:21).

There was something on the message that night that seemed to carry a greater weight of authority. God was planning something powerful. As we came to ministry time, there was a lady there who was sitting in the front area. As I looked at her, I saw God's presence move into her mouth. It has a certain look that is difficult to describe. I felt faith moving in me and declared there was a miracle in her mouth. I asked her what she needed, and she opened her mouth to show me that half of her tongue was missing. Cancer had robbed this wonderful woman of half of her tongue, and if there is one thing I absolutely want to see removed from all of mankind, it is cancer. I could sense the power and authority of Jesus was present, and just as He sent His disciples to heal the sick and do miracles in His name, I proclaimed over her that God was going to grow her tongue back by morning. The next week, I received a text message. The pastor sent a message that the next morning, the young lady with the missing tongue had woken up with her tongue completely made whole. The other half of her tongue had been restored! You see, death and life are in the power of the tongue! This was a very special miracle! As the Word was spoken on the power of the tongue, God moved a mountain in this woman's life and made her tongue whole!

The seer has another secret—**the secret power of words**. This secret is almost so obvious due to the amount of times we step into the words we have spoken on a daily basis. Whether we speak negative words or positive words, we are setting up the framework for the environment we carry. If words create worlds, they also set the tone for many of the things God wants to accomplish in our life. The struggle that seems to be a common difficulty is finding the right words to articulate the realm of the supernatural. How many times do blank stares become the common response when we are trying to convey a vision or a supernatural idea? Where is the disconnect, and how do we convey and convince others of what we are seeing? The secret power of words is our missing element.

I have been in the ministry of healing for over a decade, after having been healed of some things myself. For years I have been praying for God to use me to heal the sick of every infirmity and disease. I want to see cancers disappear as we pray, viruses to be removed, skin disorders to be healed, even the common cold to be cured as we pray. I love watching God remove the sickness so that healing can be there, yet I also believe God wants to do more than remove what is painful—He also wants to restore what is missing.

During a trip to Brazil over a decade ago, I remember praying for a young boy and his foot. One foot was normal—fully developed, with every bone and tissue necessary to support itself. The other foot was missing bone. To be honest, I don't know which bone exactly it was. It might have been a metatarsal; it might have been some other bone. We were working with the translator to bring things from Portuguese to English and English back to Portuguese. I sat there praying over this kid's foot, lamenting in my head that it was going to be a long night. I really had no thoughts other than that I was on autopilot. All the sudden, it was like I was visualizing the bone growing, but I really wasn't intentionally doing it. It was like I was daydreaming of the bone growing back. I spoke over the foot of this boy in very simple, caveman-like statements: "Be healed. Bone grow." With my hand on his foot and the interpreter by my side, I felt the bone grow back under my hand. It was like a balloon inflating under the skin, only this one had a shape and function this boy desperately needed. Clapping, hugging, and celebrating, the family and I stood there in awe of what Jesus had just done for this boy! Going back to my room that night, I tried to process what happened. It felt like I was in shock, realizing I had come that close to the Divine. I could only be in awe and give God praise.

As I reflected on this moment over the next year, I started having recurring visions of bones, missing limbs, eyeballs, and eardrums. It was strange, and yet it kept happening. I asked the Holy Spirit what they were, and what I heard back shocked me. I was being shown the missing body parts that were being saved for moments when someone by faith would bring them from Heaven to earth. I am aware that I am not the only one who has seen this same vision. We are going to see a massive awakening, and at the center of this move of God will be miracle moments the world has never seen before. Yet if all these body parts are just waiting to be brought out of Heaven, what is the delay? How do we see these miracles come to pass? This is where the seer's secret power of words brings us into another level of encounter. Words bring the invisible into visible realities.

A DIVINE PAIRING

In the chapter on the secret of imagination, we discussed how God has things. These things are the heavenly realities that have been generously given to each one of us. These things that have been given to us are now ours because Jesus unlocked the storehouse of Heaven and gave all of His children access to the vastness of the riches of Heaven. Trouble is, we don't know how to access these things! Perhaps we think it is going to be like Christmas: we are going to wake up one morning, roll downstairs, and there will be all that was promised to us under the tree! The reality is, we don't find those things externally. The Father has a sneakier delivery system that involves a pairing of the secret of imagination and the secret power of words. When the Father wants to reveal something of Heaven on the earth, God moves on us by the power of the Holy Spirit giving us ideas. Perhaps you have experienced this phenomenon. While in worship, a flood of ideas begins to fill your mind. These are not normal ideas; these are outrageous ideas—like how to end world hunger, bring hope to the masses, or restore the addicted person back into a place of health and wholeness. As we worship, we become a think tank for the Holy Spirit. Inside of our spirit-soul is the ability to hear the thoughts of Heaven. We have explored the wonder of imagination and its incredible ability to bring us into life-changing encounters with Jesus. Yet the question remains: How do I bring the invisible things going on in my heart to a place where they can be seen by the world around me? Perhaps you have heard or seen something from the Holy Spirit but do not know how to articulate it. The thing is, we often attempt to communicate the depth of what we are seeing but find ourselves using very shallow language.

> *Now we have received, not the spirit of the world, but the Spirit who is from God, so that we may know the things freely given to us by God, which things we also speak, not in words taught by human wisdom, but in those taught by the Spirit, combining spiritual thoughts with spiritual words* (1 Corinthians 2:12-13 NASB).

The divine pairing happens when we are able to marry *"spiritual thoughts with spiritual words"* (1 Cor. 2:13). As we grow, our abilities with the language of the Spirit grow as well. At first we might find ourselves struggling to find the words to accurately portray the wonder of what we have witnessed in the spirit realm. It's like trying to speak about a 3-D world using 2-D language. Yet as we grow in revelation, the divine pairing begins to come together, and our words beautifully match the wonder of spiritual thought. It is at this moment that something incredible begins to happen. When we are able to give language to the supernatural realities of which we have become aware, we begin to bring things out of 2-D and help others see what we are seeing in 3-D.

Jesus was able to do this so well. He speaks about this, saying, *"It is the Spirit who gives life; the flesh profits nothing. The words that I speak to you are spirit, and they are life"* (John 6:63). Jesus spoke spirit-life into the atmosphere with His words. He ushered spirit and life into one realm from the other through the power of His words. Spiritual realities took over the natural atmosphere as He spoke, and a different dimension called the Kingdom of God was seen and felt by those who stood by. Jesus also boldly communicates, *"You are already clean because of the word which I have spoken to you"* (John 15:3). Those who were around Jesus were spiritually made clean simply because they were present while He was talking! It is not mentioned in the Scripture, but I have no doubt that those who sat listening to Jesus teaching encountered something beyond good advice. Perhaps some went into visions of Heaven, perhaps some saw in the spirit the angelic hosts ministering with Jesus, or perhaps something else supernatural happened that caused so many to be willing to wander around in the wilderness with Jesus without a plan for food or drink. They were eating and drinking from a different reality when they heard Jesus speak. His words were so full of power that when He turns to the Roman soldiers who were clearly trained for battle, He identifies Himself as the Jesus they were seeking: *"Now when He said to them, 'I am He,' they drew back and fell to the ground"* (John 18:6). These were the soldiers that Rome had provided for the chief priest. I cannot imagine them to be week and unable, yet when these extremely intimidating band of soldiers come face to face with Jesus, the sheer force of His word overcomes every ounce of strength in which the Roman soldiers walked. Forget every picture in your memory of angry Darth Vader knocking down rebel officers with his Force powers; Jesus responds with confidence, love, hope, spirit, and life, saying "I am He," and the soldiers of Rome, the priests, and the officers are knocked down by the power of those words (see John 18:6).

Language is important. We can be sure that not all words are created equal, and at the same time conveying spiritual realities with human philosophy falls short of the glory the Holy Spirit is revealing to us. We do not speak *"in words taught by human wisdom, but in those taught by the Spirit"* (1 Cor. 2:13). Trying to convey Kingdom realities with the wisdom of this world runs us into a roadblock. Even worse, some today fall into the error of using the language of the many available religions out there because those things sound so spiritual. To "empty one's self" might sound spiritual enough to pass the litmus test, but Jesus went beyond "emptying one's self" and said, *"If anyone desires to come after Me, let him deny himself, and take up his cross, and follow Me. For whoever desires to save his life will lose it, but whoever loses his life for My sake will find it. For what profit is it to a man if he gains the whole world, and loses his own soul? Or what will a man give in exchange for his soul?"* (Matt. 16:24-26).

The seer unlocks the secret power of words by taking what God is revealing to us and communicating it in a language that can be received by those around us. Jesus spoke parables—visionary stories to convey the nature of the Kingdom. His ability to take difficult spiritual concepts and put them into a language of the culture made it something relevant to those in His day. Dreams have a way of doing this by revealing spiritual concepts to us in a language that is often deeply personal. God takes the things we are aware of and forms a dream for us using those things as code to get our attention and in the end reveals something often profoundly deep to us that requires deciphering and interpretation. There is a message within the message, and dreams are like that. Like with Jesus—you think He is talking about a recipe on how to make really fluffy bread, but really He is talking about the Kingdom. He is connecting the dots for the world to see His reality through the lens of the language of life. Are you able to connect the dots for those who are listening to you share your revelation? If we are going to be trusted to convey the mysteries of Heaven to a generation, we need to ask God for ways to break the language barrier and communicate supernatural realities in a way that will be received.

Big Block Letters

Finding words worthy to match the spiritual reality of what you are seeing may be difficult at first, but with grace and effort you begin to find ones to wrap around the vision of what it is God is showing you. Often the first couple of people with whom we share the vision may not be totally on board with everything we are saying. It's not unusual to get some blank stares in response to a massive download that the Holy Spirit just revealed in the secret place. What can often get misunderstood is that the confusion is not on their part, but on ours. Picture them as the sounding board you are using to test drive your new idea with. We may think, "Oh, this is so simple. How do they not get this?" But the problem is, what you are sharing with them is not common sense; it is supernatural. Conveying supernatural ideas takes practice. We often find ourselves in trouble, giving up so fast on something God revealed to us, because the people we just shared our God idea with are not immediately jumping in on it like it's the next big thing. Don't worry. That thing may be burning in your heart, and it may not be something they are designed by God to partner with. Instead, stay focused and refine your vision so that it can be communicated in a way that will be received with grace. How do we do this? Write it out in big block letters!

> *And then God answered: "Write this. Write what you see. Write it out in big block letters so that it can be read on the run. This vision-message is a witness pointing to what's coming. It aches for the coming—it can hardly wait! And it doesn't lie. If it seems slow in coming, wait. It's on its way. It will come right on time"* (Habakkuk 2:2 MSG).

Often our vision cannot pass the runner's test. Imagine a runner running by quickly. You are on the sidelines and want to convey something important like, "Hubby called. He wants you to pick up milk on the way home." Simple enough, but this person has to be able to read it on the run. It's time to write it in big block letters. Can you communicate in a way that the God concept is so simple that it is also memorable? When Jesus talked about the seed and the sower, these were pictures that revealed Kingdom concepts. It was a snippet, something quick and easily understood. The seer knows this and brings things down to a place where the words they speak become eyes for those who have yet to see.

VOICE ACTIVATED

> *And since we have the same spirit of faith, according to what is written, "I believed and therefore I spoke," we also believe and therefore speak* (2 Corinthians 4:13).

The secret power of words is the seer's secret to bringing invisible realities into the visible world. The world itself was framed by the word of God, and in the same way every day we have a chance to frame the future by speaking out the word God is breathing in our spirit. The invisible world is voice activated. When we believe in what God has spoken to us, faith causes us to echo His word to the world around us. Speak the vision, and let it be something that develops and forms over time like it is an organic life, growing and developing in a healthy way that is more and more understandable as the revelation matures.

KEYS TO UNLOCKING THIS SECRET

Write the vision.

Carefully putting on paper what God is speaking to us brings things from hearing to seeing. Taking it from seeing in your heart to seeing it on paper will breathe life to it and is the first step in making it visible.

Practice speaking.

Allow yourself to talk about it. If God shows you something, giving language to it is going to be something of a process. Allow it to develop as you share. It may come out at first like an uncut diamond, but as you share it the rough edges are being refined and eventually it will be something everyone is able to see and appreciate.

Study the parables.

How did Jesus convey spiritual realities? What was His main method? *"But without a parable He did not speak to them. And when they were alone, He explained all things to His disciples"* (Mark 4:34). Jesus' use of parables was not meant to trick people but to convey higher realities in a natural way. Study the parables and recognize His wisdom. Matthew 13 is full of them, short snippets that demonstrate the Kingdom. The goal is to be able to convey what we are seeing in words that make sense to everyone around us.

CHAPTER
11

THE SECRET
OF DREAMING

Hear now My words: "If there is a prophet among you, I, the Lord, make Myself known to him in a vision; I speak to him in a dream."

—NUMBERS 12:6

Dreams are the language of the last days. Maybe we should get used to the language—and not just say, "It was a dream."

—LOU ENGLE

$\mathcal{I}$ was waking up from one of the most incredible dreams I had had in a while. I could hear the sound of my son getting up from the long night and walking toward my bed. He was just about to turn three at the time. Some days he was convinced he was a T-Rex, and other days he was a lion! He was roaring down the hallway as if to announce the T-Rex had risen. His morning ritual involved roaring like a dinosaur to wake up the family. He would then pounce on me with all his dinosaur muscles, and we would wrestle out the morning! When I woke up to his roar, I could not remember the dream I had just had. I knew it was an important one so I stayed quiet, trying to remember the dream. Realizing I had less than a minute until my son would jump on top of me to wake me up, I laid there perfectly still, attempting to faintly recall anything I could from the dream. My son's roar getting closer and closer, I realized I may not get the dream back because I was about to come face to face with a two-and-a-half-foot T-Rex who would wonderfully distract me from my dream! As he was turning into my room, I realized I was not going to remember the dream so I might as well stand to my feet to greet my little T-Rex. When I stood up to look at my boy, in the middle of the room in between us was an angel sitting there, looking at me with a huge smile on his face! He was wearing soldier's armor that reminded me of a Roman centurion. As I looked at him in absolute shock, my dream immediately came back to me! The angel before me was also in the dream showing me things that would forever change my life. It all flooded back into my memory, and I recalled every detail of the dream as if the angel was there to make sure I remembered how important it really was. When I recalled the dream, the angel immediately disappeared.

According to a group of French researchers writing in the *Journal of Sleep Research*, "Dreaming production is universal, while dreaming recall is variable."[20] Everyone dreams, but the ability to remember

our dreams is an entirely different thing. This brings us to the last
secret of the seer—**the secret of dreaming**. Dream recall is the ability to remember our dreams. I was dreaming from as early as I can
remember, having vivid dreams of flying and other incredible things.
Dreams are strange in that they defy most everything we know to
be true. In life we are earth bound by the weight of gravity, yet in
dreams we can fly! Breathing underwater is an impossibility that
often seems only natural in a dream. Why does God speak to us in
such opposites? Perhaps He is trying to get our attention!

The secret of dreaming is the mystery that everyone dreams, yet
not everyone remembers. Jesus even confronted the disciples about
their inability to remember the God moment they shared together
only hours earlier: *"Having eyes, do you not see? And having ears, do
you not hear? And do you not remember?"* (Mark 8:18). The ability to
remember is more spiritual than we realize. I would even propose
that spiritual memory needs to be worked out like a muscle, just as
much as our natural memory. This practice of memory increases our
spiritual development. Jesus warned to be on guard that the enemy
will steal the word when we are not receiving it well: *"When anyone
hears the word of the kingdom, and does not understand it, then the wicked
one comes and snatches away what was sown in his heart. This is he who
received seed by the wayside"* (Matt. 13:19). Remembering our dreams is
vital to hearing the word that God speaks. If He is truly speaking to
us in our dreams, and if we all dream, are there any ways to increase
our ability to remember?

When I realized the importance of my dreams and that God was
really inserting Himself into my dream life, I began to pay attention and practice remembering my dreams. It might have been the
middle of the night, but I would wake up to write the dreams down.
I noticed when I began to do this that dreams began to increase in
their frequency. More and more I would find myself waking up in

the morning with entire stories to tell of dreams that happened while sleeping. It was like a whole new world had opened to me, and now I was fascinated with dreams and their ability to connect me to the heart of God.

Remembering something is committing that thing to memory. This happens when we take a moment to honor the importance that God really did speak to me to in a dream. When you and I take time to commit to memory the details and the big-picture ideas that God gave us in the dream, something happens that demonstrates to God our willingness to be faithful with what He is revealing to us. Faithfulness is key to this secret.

> *For whoever has, to him more will be given, and he will have abundance; but whoever does not have, even what he has will be taken away from him* (Matthew 13:12).

As we faithfully observe what we have been given, more will come and we will begin to unlock the secret of dreaming. Everyone dreams. It is the faithfulness to put the dream in a place that can be remembered that awakens the ability of dream recall. This ability to remember is like a muscle: the more we use it, the stronger it will be.

DREAMS & VISIONS

> *For God may speak in one way, or in another, yet man does not perceive it. In a **dream**, in **a vision of the night, when deep sleep falls upon men, while slumbering on their beds**, then He opens the ears of men, and seals their instruction. In order to turn man from his deed, and conceal pride from man* (Job 33:14-17).

Dreams and visions are the language we hear from God while sleeping. There is a simple way to increase the chances of having dreams and visions: sleep more often! An old seer prophet I once knew would say to people, "You want me to take a nap." He was not posing a question; rather, he was suggesting something that he knew would increase the chances of God speaking to him something important. He knew if those around him would allow him to sleep, he would probably have a dream or vision from God that would bless those he was with.

If everyone dreams, what is it that keeps us from recalling? The message in the Book of Job tells us that dreams are often concealed from our memories due to the pride of man. When we have a dream and we cannot recall it, sometimes it is because God is hiding the dream upon waking so that we do not fall into pride. What would pride look like when it comes to a dream? Pride causes us to do something in our own strength instead of walking with Jesus through the process. Once we have a dream and we understand it, avoiding pride means we immediately turn our heart and mind to God, asking Him how we can partner with Him through the process. Pride skips this step and makes the mistake of trying to do it on our own. I have had dreams that informed me of something going on in someone's life, and instead of going to God in prayer about it, I immediately went to that person to talk to them about it. This backfired immediately and did not produce any fruit. For me, God gave me the dream to better pray for that person, but skipping a step caused me to fall into pride. What are some ways that we can increase the chances of remembering our dreams? Here are some perspectives and practices that I have found increase dream recall and grant us the ability to receive what God is giving to us in our dreams.

DREAM JOURNALS

A dream journal is a great tool to keep this seer secret. Paying attention to sleep quality, length of sleep, and timing of dreams might give you a clue as to what to expect as you record details of your night seasons. Sleeping becomes a place of encounter, and as you place value on your sleep by observing the details of it, something begins to happen with the frequency of heavenly activity in the night. Dreams become more frequent, and seer encounters and visions that once seemed too "out there" become a more normal part of your sleep history. In the sleep journal, you write out little things that come to your mind in the night. Little downloads of revelation are given a place of honor by putting them in writing. I have musician friends who hear songs from Heaven in their sleep—often lyrics that become a springboard for the next worship song they release. Pay attention to these things and value them by writing them down as fast as is doable.

Record your dreams and write them down. Putting them on paper does something to help us realize the meaning of the dream. It seems that as we write them down, something begins to happen that makes them easier to understand. I like to write my visions, dreams, and seer encounters down and meditate on them throughout the day. If there is something I am unable to understand about it, I will go to the Scripture to find out if there is already something in there that might give insight into the meaning of something. For instance, if I see the number seven in a dream, I will immediately look up the scriptural references regarding this number. Numbers are constantly recognized in the Scripture as symbolic and intentional. As we look up the number seven, we find the first mention is of course the time when God rested from all His creative work on the seventh day. He completed His work and rested in it. As we look throughout Scripture, we find Hebrews 6:1-2 tells us six foundational elements of our faith, yet the writer encourages us to "go on toward completion," or in other words, to the seventh element (see Heb. 6:1). This theme is sown throughout the entire Scripture and gives us context to receive numbers as a code through which God communicates to us. From the scriptural evidence, seven is a number that speaks of completion and perfection. Simply writing this type of discovery in our dream journal helps us to learn and value the language of Holy Spirit. Make it simple, and you will see more of God in your sleep than ever before.

SLEEP QUALITY

Unless the Lord builds a house, its builders labor over it in vain; unless the Lord watches over a city, the watchman stays alert in vain. In vain you get up early and stay up late, working hard to have enough food—yes, He gives sleep to the one He loves (Psalm 127:1-2 HCSB).

Sleep quality is a big deal to every seer. It affects the frequency of dreams. Setting yourself up for some high quality Zs will give you the maximum advantage for seer encounters as dreams, visions, trances, and many other prophetic experiences happen while sleeping. While many might think the more spiritual you are, the more you stay awake through the night, this is absolutely not the entire truth. While there are moments to keep the watch of the Lord (which I wrote about in my book, *Supernatural Revolution*), there are other times when it is wonderfully spiritual to sleep. What very few, if anyone, will tell you is that there are times during prayer that God actually puts you to sleep! I have been praying, worshiping, and in the middle of prayer felt this unusual peace causing sleepiness. This may sound totally opposite to everything you have heard. Someone would likely tell you, "Push through," or "Fight it and pray," but because I am curious I am willing to test it and see what happens if I do allow myself to take a power nap in those moments. To my surprise, I have discovered that in those moments, I enter into a high-level seer moment. Sometimes I dream, while other times I fall into a trance or a vision. Other times, a visitation happens that is more life changing than anything I could have done in my own strength by trying to press through and fight the grace of rest that God was giving me.

Someone once walked up to me after a meeting to tell me a testimony. I was thrilled to hear the incredible story of what she wanted to share. She began the story by saying that she had been reading a book I had written and had an unusual supernatural encounter while reading it. Intrigued, I leaned in, waiting to hear the encounter. She continued, telling me that she was reading and while in the middle of the book, she fell asleep. I responded, laughing, "Oh wow! It was that good, eh?" She continued, "Oh no, it was what happened after this. I have never had this happen before. When I fell asleep, I could hear the sound of wind whipping all around me. It was the Holy Spirit. His presence was moving in and around me, and I was caught up into a realm of the presence of God like I had never experienced before in my life!" I was relieved it was not the book making her sleep! It was the presence of God!

Without a doubt, we are one of the most heavily caffeinated generations. There are hundreds, if not thousands, of ways to drink yourself awake. Personally, it seems coffee with a touch of cream makes me a much better Christian! Yet at the end of every night is the dreaded sleep issue. As a proud parent of two night walkers (zombie children), I have learned that sleep may be one of the most profound gifts of all. Society has traditionally shamed and belittled the person who sleeps in, labeling them as "lazy" and "unmotivated." The traditional thought of "late to bed and early to rise" makes an insomniac seem like the most spiritual person. Sleep may be one of the most undervalued parts of life, yet we spend one-third of our life practicing this gift. If I told you that you were biologically forced to do something one-third of your day, would you want to get really great at it? Here we come to one of the most vital secrets of the seer—the secret of dreaming. Personally, I want to excel at sleep. I want to be excellent at naps, sleep through the night, and treasure this wonderful gift God has given me. This might sound completely unspiritual and perhaps even come off as immature, but even companies like Google understand sleep's vital role in the health of their employees' creativity. EnergyPods are part of the décor at the Google campus because Google knows that to keep their creative teams at high energy, it takes a lot more than coffee. Inside of those pods, employees rest in the optimum position for blood flow so they can stay fresh and alert and maintain the highest level of productivity! As a high doer, I often feel guilty sleeping in or taking a nap, but I have discovered that the most profound encounters I have had with God happen when I sleep with the expectation of connecting with Him.

Everyone sleeps, but not everyone sleeps with the intention of experiencing the realm of the supernatural. Yet God designed sleep as a way not just to recharge the body, but to give vision to our heart. Many of the seer encounters throughout Scripture were described as happening while dreaming. Daniel is a dreamer who received some of the most revelatory insights into the things of God through dreams.

> *And I heard a man's voice between the banks of the Ulai, who called, and said, "Gabriel, make this man understand the vision." So he came near where I stood, and when he came I was afraid and fell on my face; but he said to me, "Understand, son of man, that the vision refers to the time of the end."* ***Now, as he was speaking with me, I was in a deep sleep with my face to the ground;*** *but he touched me, and stood me upright* (Daniel 8:16-18).

This one amazes me. It is as if the weight of this encounter can be received only in a dream. The archangel Gabriel brings a message to Daniel, yet Daniel is face first on the ground in a deep sleep. The angel touches him, and this touch strengthens him enough to stand up under the weight of the glory being encountered in that moment.

SLEEPING AWAKE

I sleep, but my heart is awake; it is the voice of my beloved!
He knocks, saying, "Open for me, my sister, my love, My
dove, my perfect one; for my head is covered with dew, my
locks with the drops of the night" (Song of Solomon 5:2).

From a biblical and spiritual perspective, sleep is an activity wherein your body is asleep but the spirit is awake. Practicing the secret of dreaming means that we sleep with the intention of allowing our body to rest and pay attention with our spirit. I can sleep knowing full well that my body needs the rest, but I can also pay attention with my spirit and have my mind fixed with expectation that God is going to speak to me. Sleeping awake is the practice of going to bed with an expectation for dreams.

DREAM ROOMS

I was going to stay with some friends on a recent trip, and they picked me up at the airport and noticed how exhausted I was. I had just returned from an out-of-country trip and was feeling the difficulty of jet lag. Everything in me was crying out for a chance to sleep. When we arrived at their house, their encouragement to me was, "Feel free to take a nap." Respectfully, I accepted their offer! "Please lead me to my room," I said. When we got to the room, the bed looked like something out of an interior design magazine. I didn't get a total count of the pillows on the bed, but my best guess is that there were more than a dozen. This thing was spectacular. My host graciously gave me the room, and she and her husband retreated to the other side of the house.

Just as I was about to shut the door, one of them told me I should expect heavenly encounters while sleeping in that room. Now, I have heard this before. Someone maybe once had a dream or seer encounter that profoundly impacted their life, and what happens is we memorialize this place as sacred space. This might sound cliché, but it really is not off-the-wall thinking. In fact, this is what Jacob did at Bethel. As I laid my head down on the bed and drifted off to sleep, I was in no mood to have an encounter with God. That might sound completely unspiritual, but I was so tired that the only thing I wanted in that moment was a solid two hours of uninterrupted sleep. When I closed my eyes on that big comfy bed with those massive pillows surrounding me, I drifted off into a deep sleep that my body desperately needed. Waking up was wild because I could remember that I had just fallen asleep in a big comfy bed, but when I woke up I was now in a place with crystal-clear water! This was not a place on earth but a seer encounter with Heaven. While my body was sleeping, my spirit man was encountering something supernatural. The Lord Jesus was with me in this place, and we were splashing around in this water that I knew was the water of life that John the revelator saw in the Book of Revelation. *"And he showed me a pure river of water of life, clear as crystal, proceeding from the throne of God and of the Lamb"* (Rev. 22:1). Within a moment, I was awake—and this time in the bedroom in which I had fallen asleep. What seemed like a moment in Heaven was in actuality close to two hours in the physical world! Seer encounters, including dreams and visions, often happen while sleeping and may happen when you least expect it. Certain places and spaces seem to have an ability to enter us into dreaming and visions with ease.

> *So he came to a certain place and stayed there all night, because the sun had set. And he took one of the stones of that place and put it at his head, and he lay down in that place to*

sleep. Then he dreamed, and behold, a ladder was set up on the earth, and its top reached to heaven; and there the angels of God were ascending and descending on it. And behold, the Lord stood above it.... Then Jacob awoke from his sleep and said, "Surely the Lord is in this place, and I did not know it" (Genesis 28:11-13b,16).

Simply looking for a place to rest, God invades Jacob's sleep with a dream that would forever change the course of history. After waking, Jacob renamed that place Bethel, meaning "house of God." *"And he was afraid and said, 'How awesome is this place! This is none other than the house of God, and this is the gate of heaven!'"* (Gen. 28:17). Sleeping in that place gives Jacob the ability to dream vividly and see what the Lord is doing.

Before you go to sleep, whether in a hotel or your own room, dedicate the place of your rest as an area consecrated for God to speak to you in dreams. Speak this prayer over your bedroom:

> *Father, let this place be a sanctuary for dreams and visions from Your Spirit. In this place, let my ears hear, my eyes see, and my heart understand all You desire to share with me while I sleep. I thank You for incredible, quality sleep and receive the dreams You have for me. Protect me from every evil while I sleep, and may I only hear Your thoughts toward me! In Jesus' name. Amen!*

KEYS TO UNLOCKING THIS SECRET

Keep a dream journal.

Having a dream journal is an incredible way to keep track of your dreams. Keeping it next to your bed will make it convenient to write the dream down directly after having it. I like to use my phone as a way of journaling my dreams. There are plenty of apps that have the ability to keep your writings forever in the digital cloud. I like it this method of journaling because then there is not much need to turn on the light and look around for a pen.

Practice quality sleep.

Getting quality rest will increase the chances of remembering your dreams. If I am starving for sleep, I usually just roll over and go back to bed after having a dream. If I am practicing good sleep habits, like paying attention to my body's need to sleep, I will be more apt to remember my dreams and also enjoy the times when I am dreaming. Practicing quality sleep is sowing and reaping. Having great dreams is reaping from what I have sown into it.

Pray before sleeping.

Praying before bed is not something that is only for children. Inviting the Father, Son, and Holy Spirit into your dream life is vital to unlocking the secret of dreaming. Let God know that you desire to hear from Him, and practice praying the prayer in the last section as part of your routine before you go to sleep. Ask God to visit you in the night seasons and you will activate a world of dreaming with God!

CHAPTER
12

ACTIVATION OF SEER REVELATION

Behold, I stand at the door and knock. If anyone hears My voice and opens the door, I will come in to him and dine with him, and he with Me.

—REVELATION 3:20

You may be wondering, "What's next? I have read this book and am wondering where I go from here?" *Secrets of the Seer* is a book filled with practices and perspectives that put you in the pathway for seer encounters. Many people with whom I have spoken come to me asking, "Jamie, I want to have dreams and visions too! I want angelic encounters! What do I do?" Here is the thing: the nature of every heavenly encounter is designed to bring us closer to Jesus. It is given so that we may know the ways of God and experience Him from a new perspective. When an angel from God does appear to me, the first thing going through my head is, "Take me to your Leader!" I want a deeper revelation of God. And if you look through the encounters in Scripture, you will find that the greatest up close and personal encounters with God were given to reveal who He really is. The first seer encounter of Moses started with God revealing who He is. Moses wanted to know whom He was talking with, *"and God said to Moses, 'I AM WHO I AM.' And He said, 'Thus you shall say to the children of Israel, "I AM has sent me to you"'"* (Exod. 3:14).

For many years, the Book of Revelation has been picked apart as "the Revelation of the End Times," "the Revelation of the Antichrist," or "the Revelation of the Mark of the Beast." I have sat through message after message where people are trying to comb through the Scriptures to discover what the Book of Revelation is, attempting to tell us about this or that. But the opening line in the Book of Revelation tells us exactly what—or who—it is revealing to us: ***"The Revelation of Jesus Christ**, which God gave Him to show His servants—things which must shortly take place. **And He sent and signified it by His angel to His servant John"*** (Rev. 1:1). Whether having an angelic encounter, a vision, a trance, a dream, an out-of-body experience, it should be experienced with the one desire of knowing Jesus.

He stands at the door and knocks (see Rev. 3:20). These practices and perspectives are ways to embrace the knocking in our life. He longs to speak to us through dreams, visions, and third heaven encounters. He loves to show off Heaven to us. So then, we *"seek those things which are above, where Christ is, sitting at the right hand of God"* (Col. 3:1b).

When I think of these "secrets," they are like keys that are used to unlock supernatural realities. Jesus said to Peter, *"And I will give you the keys of the kingdom of heaven, and whatever you bind on earth will be bound in heaven, and whatever you loose on earth will be loosed in heaven"* (Matt. 16:19). The keys were not just binding and loosing. So many people really misunderstand the keys Jesus is speaking about here. He is promising Peter keys to spiritual realities that, when used, would activate Heaven on earth. Later Jesus reveals one of the greatest keys of all to Peter—the key of forgiveness.

> *Then Peter came to Him and said, "Lord, how often shall my brother sin against me, and I forgive him? Up to seven times?" Jesus said to him, "I do not say to you, up to seven times, but up to seventy times seven"* (Matthew 18:21-22).

This key was once a mystery so difficult for the people in that day to grasp that Jesus likened it to the difficulty of moving a tree out of the ground and into the ocean simply by speaking to it. *"'Take heed to yourselves. If your brother sins against you, rebuke him; and if he repents, forgive him. And if he sins against you seven times in a day, and seven times in a day returns to you, saying, "I repent," you shall forgive him.' And the apostles said to the Lord, 'Increase our faith'"* (Luke 17:3-5). They needed faith—the kind of faith that could move mountains, the kind of faith to do the impossible—simply to use the key of forgiveness. It was up to them as to how they wanted to use the key! Would they bind or loose? Would they partner with Heaven to use the key in the way it was intended by God? Every pop psychology book today makes forgiveness a basic principle, but Jesus was presenting something brand new and the disciples needed faith to step into it.

I want to partner right now with your faith to receive supernatural encounters with Heaven. I ask that you pray a prayer with me that was spoken by the seer prophet Elisha, who prayed for his sidekick to see the armies of the living God who were standing to fight on their behalf:

> *And Elisha prayed, and said, "Lord, I pray, open his eyes that he may see." Then the Lord opened the eyes of the young man, and he saw. And behold, the mountain was full of horses and chariots of fire all around Elisha* (2 Kings 6:17).

Pray this with me:

> *Father, I ask that You would open my eyes that I may see. Give me ears to hear, eyes to see, and a heart to understand! I step into seer encounters with You by faith. May my dreams be filled with revelation from Your heart to mine. I receive visions of Your love and the mysteries of the Kingdom of Heaven given by Your Spirit. Let the angelic hosts of Heaven declare Your goodness to me. Let my eyes see Your glory and may my whole body, soul, and spirit be filled with Your light! In Jesus' name I ask this. Amen and Amen.*

NOTES

1. "Appointment," *The Merriam-Webster Learner's Dictionary*, www
   .learnersdictionary.com/definition/appointment.

2. "Disappointment," *The Merriam-Webster Learner's Dictionary*, www.
   learnersdictionary.com/definition/disappointment.

3. "Intellectual Property," *The Merriam-Webster Dictionary*, www
   .merriam-webster.com/dictionary/intellectual%20property.

4. "Strong's H7200," *Blue Letter Bible*, http://www.blueletterbible
   .org/lang/lexicon/lexicon.cfm?t=kjv&strongs=h7200.

5. Aristotle, *On the Heavens*, trans. J. L. Stocks, II.14, in *The Works of
   Aristotle*, vol. 2 (Oxford: Oxford UP, 1930), 297-98.

6. See https://wiki.tfes.org/The_Conspiracy_for_more_information_
   about_"the_flat_earth_conspiracy."

7. "Bilocation," *The Merriam-Webster Dictionary*, http://www
   .merriam-webster.com/dictionary/bilocation.

8. Origen, *The Works of Origen*, vol. 1, trans. Rev. Frederick Crombie
   (London: Hamilton, 1869), 144.

9. Gregory Thaumaturgus, *The Sacred Writings of Gregory Thaumaturgus*
   (Altenmünster, Germany: Jazzybee Verlag, 2012), http://books.google.
   com/books?id=x2Z5vAbXAIwC.

10. St. Antony the Great qtd. in St. Nikodimos, *The Philokalia*, vol. 1,
    trans. and ed. G. E. H. Palmer, Philip Sherrard, and Kallistos Ware
    (Boston: Faber and Faber, 1979), 338.

11. St. John Climacus qtd. in Father Joseph Irvin, ed., *The Church Fathers
    Speak*, An Inquirer's Guide to Orthodox Christianity 12 (United
    States: CreateSpace, 2017), 28.

12. Lynne Blumberg, "What Happens to the Brain During
    Spiritual Experiences?" *The Atlantic*, last modified June 5,
    2014, https://www.theatlantic.com/health/archive/2014/06/
    what-happens-to-brains-during-spiritual-experiences/361882/.

13. "Strong's Concordance 3045," *Biblehub.com*, http://biblehub.com/hebrew/3045.htm.

14. Mona Lisa Chanda and Daniel J. Levitin, "The Neurochemistry of Music," *Trends in Cognitive Science* 17, no. 4 (April 2013): 179-93. PDF, http://daniellevitin.com/levitinlab/articles/2013-TICS_1180.pdf.

15. Elizabeth Landau, "This Is Your Brain on Music," *CNN.com*, last modified February 2, 2016, http://www.cnn.com/ 2013/04/15/health/brain-music-research/index.html.

16. Helena Merriman, "The Blind Boy Who Learned to See with Sound," *BBC.com*, last modified February 12, 2016, http://www.bbc.com/news/disability-35550768.

17. Fabrice Dosseville, Sylvain Laborde, and Nicolas Scelles, "Music During Lectures: Will Studies Learn Better?" *Learning and Individual Differences* 22 (2012): 258-62.

18. Mazlan, "The Effect of Music on Plant Growth," *Den Garden* (blog), last modified May 23, 2017, http://dengarden.com/gardening/the-effect-of-music-on-plant-growth.

19. "How Mozart's Music Is Improving the Grapes in One Italian Vineyard," *CBS.com*, last modified January 2, 2017, http://www.cbsnews.com/news/mozart-classical-music-helps-grapes-grow-italy-vineyard/.

20. B. Herlin et al., "Evidence That Non-dreamers Do Dream: A REM Sleep Behaviour Disorder Model," *Journal of Sleep Research* 24, no. 6 (2015): 602-09.

About the Author

*J*amie Galloway carries a revival message that imparts a lifestyle of the supernatural. He has a broad ministry experience from planting churches to speaking at stadium events. He is a sought after prophetic communicator and is involved in various media projects that highlight the move of God for our generation.

SECRETS

OF THE *Seer*

E-COURSE

DIVE DEEPER INTO ACTIVATING A SEER LIFESTYLE

Let Jamie take you step-by-step through an exploration of the Ten Secrets in this user friendly online E-Course. Join others and jump into an online learning experience designed to activate a lifestyle of Seer Encounters. Also, enjoy a free message on Heavenly encounters at the web link below.

jamiegalloway.com/secrets